MY FA____

CHAPTER I.

EARLY LIFE AND PROGRESS AS A SEAMAN.

SECTION I.—*My Father's early Life.*

THE name of SCORESBY, it is believed, is entirely unknown, in this country, except in the case of the family, and one or two relations, of the subject of the present records.

My Father's "more immediate ancestors," as a short biographical account of him by a friend, states,* "occupied respectable stations in the middle walks of life, supporting, in each case, unblemished character, and possessing, at times, considerable property;" and, in periods rather remote, holding conspicuous stations.

In Drake's History of York, the family name, varying in the spelling in a progress through several centuries, repeatedly occurs. But the single line traceable through my Father's ancestors, now alone appears to exist in Britain. Walter de Scourby was

---

* " Memoir of William Scoresby, Esq." by the late Mr. Samuel Drew, in the "Imperial Magazine," for 1822.

"bayliffe of York," in the year 1312; and in the seventh and ninth years of Edward III., Nicholas de Scorēby, it appears, was Member for York. Subsequently, we find, under the date of 1463, Thomas Scawsby, holding the office of Lord Mayor of that city. Some member of the family, after the name assumed its present form, must have given the designation of "Scoresby Manor" and "Scoresby Lodge," to places still known in the neighbourhood of York.

At the period, however, of this memoir, the family occupied more humble stations in life, chiefly in the class of yeomen,—a class once of much importance in this country, but now, unhappily, so diminished in numbers, under the absorbing influence of extensive properties, as to be scarcely recognised as a designation.

William Scoresby, my Father, 'was born on the 3d of May 1760, on a small estate farmed by his parent, called Nutholm, in the township of Cropton, about twenty miles south-west of Whitby, in the county of York. In this place the periods of his childhood and boyhood were spent.'

The memoir, here again quoted, refers to some incidents among his earliest recollections, by which his life was greatly imperilled, marking 'the superintending providence of God, which, on all occasions, he gratefully acknowledged.'

At an endowed school, in the nearest adjoining village, Cropton, his early, and indeed chief, education was received. But the distance being considerable,

CAMBRIDGE LIBRARY COLLECTION

Books of enduring scholarly value

Polar Exploration

This series includes accounts, by eye-witnesses and contemporaries, of early expeditions to the Arctic and the Antarctic. Huge resources were invested in such endeavours, particularly the search for the North-West Passage, which, if successful, promised enormous strategic and commercial rewards. Cartographers and scientists travelled with many of the expeditions, and their work made important contributions to earth sciences, climatology, botany and zoology. They also brought back anthropological information about the indigenous peoples of the Arctic region and the southern fringes of the American continent. The series further includes dramatic and poignant accounts of the harsh realities of working in extreme conditions and utter isolation in bygone centuries.

Memorials of the Sea: My Father

Son of an Arctic whaler, William Scoresby (1789–1857) made the first of many voyages to northern latitudes when he was just ten years old. Later a scientist and clergyman, he wrote on a wide range of topics, and his observations on the Arctic prompted further exploration of the region. He published some of his accounts under the generic title of 'Memorials of the Sea' (his 1835 notes on murder at sea and on the fate of the Franklin expedition have also been reissued in this series). In this 1851 book, Scoresby recounts the life of his father, also William (1760–1829), from his earliest days to his later life as a prosperous captain and exceptional navigator in the Arctic whale-fisheries, at a period when the industry gave rise to extreme danger but also offered enormous financial rewards. William junior's biography is also available in the Cambridge Library Collection.

Cambridge University Press has long been a pioneer in the reissuing of out-of-print titles from its own backlist, producing digital reprints of books that are still sought after by scholars and students but could not be reprinted economically using traditional technology. The Cambridge Library Collection extends this activity to a wider range of books which are still of importance to researchers and professionals, either for the source material they contain, or as landmarks in the history of their academic discipline.

Drawing from the world-renowned collections in the Cambridge University Library and other partner libraries, and guided by the advice of experts in each subject area, Cambridge University Press is using state-of-the-art scanning machines in its own Printing House to capture the content of each book selected for inclusion. The files are processed to give a consistently clear, crisp image, and the books finished to the high quality standard for which the Press is recognised around the world. The latest print-on-demand technology ensures that the books will remain available indefinitely, and that orders for single or multiple copies can quickly be supplied.

The Cambridge Library Collection brings back to life books of enduring scholarly value (including out-of-copyright works originally issued by other publishers) across a wide range of disciplines in the humanities and social sciences and in science and technology.

Memorials of the Sea: My Father

Being Records of the Adventurous Life of the Late William Scoresby, Esq. of Whitby

WILLIAM SCORESBY

CAMBRIDGE
UNIVERSITY PRESS

CAMBRIDGE
UNIVERSITY PRESS

University Printing House, Cambridge, CB2 8BS, United Kingdom

Cambridge University Press is part of the University of Cambridge.
It furthers the University's mission by disseminating knowledge in the pursuit of
education, learning and research at the highest international levels of excellence.

www.cambridge.org
Information on this title: www.cambridge.org/9781108081795

© in this compilation Cambridge University Press 2019

This edition first published 1851
This digitally printed version 2019

ISBN 978-1-108-08179-5 Paperback

My Father.

MEMORIALS OF THE SEA.

My Father:

BEING RECORDS OF THE ADVENTUROUS LIFE
OF THE LATE

WILLIAM SCORESBY, ESQ.

OF WHITBY.

BY HIS SON

THE REV. WILLIAM SCORESBY, D.D.

FELLOW OF THE ROYAL SOCIETIES OF LONDON AND EDINBURGH;
MEMBER OF THE INSTITUTE OF FRANCE; OF THE
AMERICAN INSTITUTE, PHILADELPHIA,
ETC. ETC.

LONDON:

LONGMAN, BROWN, GREEN, AND LONGMANS.

1851.

TO THE LADY MATILDA MAXWELL,

WHOSE DISCERNMENT OF AN UNUSUAL AND SUPERIOR
CHARACTER IN A MERCHANT SEAMAN,
WHEN KNOWN ONLY BY REPORT,
FIRST LED TO THE GATHERING OF RECORDS
CONCERNING HIM;

AND TO WHOSE EXPRESSIONS
OF DEEP AND ADMIRING INTEREST IN THE RELATION,
REPEATEDLY SOLICITED,
OF MANY CHARACTERISTIC INCIDENTS,
THEIR PUBLICATION IS STRICTLY DUE,—

𝕿𝖍𝖎𝖘 𝖁𝖔𝖑𝖚𝖒𝖊,

COMPRISING THE OFT-TOLD STORIES, WITH
ADDITIONAL RECORDS,
OF THE ADVENTUROUS LIFE OF

𝕳𝖎𝖘 𝕱𝖆𝖙𝖍𝖊𝖗,

IS, WITH GREAT RESPECT AND SINCERE REGARD,
NOW ADDRESSED,

BY HER LADYSHIP'S

FAITHFUL AND OBLIGED FRIEND,

THE AUTHOR.

Torquay, Feb. 3, 1851.

𝕸𝖞 𝕱𝖆𝖙𝖍𝖊𝖗.

CONTENTS.

MEMORIALS OF THE SEA.

My Father.

and the roads indifferent, his attendance was much interrupted, and, in winter, totally suspended. His progress, therefore, was far from being satisfactory. Nor was this disadvantage compensated by any long continuance of opportunities for obtaining scholastic instruction; for, at the age of nine, he was removed, and from that time forward employed, as his strength and years might qualify him, in occupations among the cattle, and about the farm.

Occasionally, during his advance towards manhood, he was engaged with the neighbouring farmers, when, during such occupation, an incident, of *apparently* no material importance, occurred, which constituted, under the ordering of an allwise and gracious Providence, the grand turning-point in his destiny, from a probable ordinary and unobserved occupation, to a stirring, adventurous and conspicuous life. The change was induced by some unpleasant treatment he received from the family with whom he was residing. He became disgusted with a position which, without satisfying the natural capabilities and enterprise of his mind, exposed him to such indignities. The idea had, probably, been often in his mind before; but he now first resolved on leaving the occupation for which his father had destined him, and on trying at the nearest sea-port, Whitby, the adventure of a seafaring life.

It is somewhat curious that the course of life, in respect to the adoption of a seafaring profession, of two individuals,—Captain Cook and my Father,—

whose names are associated with much of interest in
the history of Whitby, and who became, in their relative degrees, conspicuous as adventurous seamen,—
turned upon apparently trifling incidents; and, as to
the exciting of feelings of disgust with their previous
occupations, of a similar character.

James Cook, like my Father, was, in early youth,
employed along with his father, in agricultural
labours.* His turn of mind, however, being suited to
something requiring more tact than the ordinary toils
in which farmers' boys were wont to be engaged,
he was removed from the work of the field to that of
the counter, with the view of learning the business of
a country shopkeeper. It was at the fishing town of
Staiths, about ten miles north-west of Whitby, and
at the shop of a Mr. W. Sanderson, haberdasher,
where Cook, at the age of sixteen or seventeen,
entered on his new employment; and it was whilst
there that the incident, which led to his abandonment
of domestic trade for sea-life, occurred.

It happened, as the early record goes, that, at a
period when the coinage generally in circulation was
much defaced and worn, a new and fresh looking
shilling was paid in by a customer. Cook, attracted
by the comparative beauty of the coin, and thinking
with regret of its going forth again in the ordinary
progress of business, substituted the sterling value,
and appropriated the new coin, as "a pocket-piece,"
to himself. It was ill-advised that he did so without

* Life of Captain James Cook, by the Rev. G. Young, of Whitby.

previously asking permission or intimating his purpose; for the shilling had been observed by his
master, its abstraction was detected, and Cook was
suspected and charged with dishonesty,—a charge
which the production of the shilling from his pocket
seemed to confirm. His keen sense of right feeling,
and of what was due to himself, rendered this incident
so painful, that he determined, if he could get
permission to do so, to leave his employment, as a
shopkeeper, and, indulging a strongly imbibed pre-
possession, turn to the sea. The unmerited suffering
was abundantly compensated by that good and
gracious Providence, whose dispensations reach to
the humblest, and specially regards the oppressed.
The young shopkeeper—turned apparently by this
fretful incident from his monotonous pursuits, and
stimulated to seek an adventurous profession, and not
opposed, but kindly aided, by his master, who had
become perfectly satisfied of his integrity—was led
into those paths of distinction whereby he became so
highly conspicuous, if not chief among the circum-
navigators of the globe!

"It is worthy of remark," says Dr. Young, in his
life of Cook, "that the coin which so forcibly attracted
his notice was what is called a *South-sea* shilling, of
the coinage of George I., marked on the reverse
s.s.c., for *South-sea Company;* as if the name of the
piece had been intended to indicate the principal
fields of his future discoveries."

If the result of disgust at his experienced indignity

turned not to account, with my Father, in so eminent a degree,—it yet was so over-ruled for good as to place him at the head of the adventurers engaged in the whale-fishery of the Greenland seas, and to render his example, perseverance, and talent, highly beneficial to his country in the furtherance of that, then, extremely important branch of national enterprise.

It was in the winter of 1779-80, that my Father proceeded to carry his resolve into effect, by leaving his place and travelling to Whitby. Guided by the suggestions of a relative, to whom he had communicated his intentions, he was recommended to Mr. Chapman,—an opulent and respectable ship-owner, and a member of the Society of Friends,—with whom he engaged himself to serve as an apprentice, for three years, in a ship called the Jane, commanded by a son of the owner.

As his services, however, were not required till the ensuing spring,—because of the practice, as to ships trading to the Baltic and Archangel, "of laying them up" for the winter,—he returned immediately home, informed his father of what he had done, and then, at his suggestion, went back to the farm he had somewhat abruptly left, and there remained until his place could be satisfactorily supplied. This being speedily accomplished, he set himself arduously to work to the studying, by the help of whatever suitable books he could get hold of, of the subjects connected with his new profession.

On the 1st of February 1780, according to previous

arrangement, he repaired to Whitby for the ratification of his agreement, and for receiving directions as to when and how his services would be required. His anxiety on this occasion, to proceed with his studies in the manner in which he found himself making gradual and encouraging progress, led him at once into an adventure of much peril, and into circumstances in which his acquirements in the *principles* of navigation had their first, yet most successful and important, application.

Finding that his services would not be required until the month of April, he determined, being full of ardour for self-improvement, not to lose a single day; so that, although the afternoon had arrived before he finished his arrangements with Mr. Chapman, he set out on his pedestrian course towards the Moors, intending to sleep at the village of Sleights. Urged, however, by his feelings, and tempted by the fineness of the evening, and the brilliant sunset, by which the distant hills (then covered with snow) were illumined and gilded, he resolved on proceeding to Salter Gate, a position, in the midst of the Moors, eight miles further in advance, and attainable only by a not very well-defined line of road across a heath-clad and totally uninhabited country. It was a region, therefore, of complete desolateness, through which he prepared to pass, and, on occasions of snow-storms, one of great danger to any travellers who might be unfortunately overtaken by them whilst in the midst of the Moors;—for, at the period of which we now write, there were neither fences to confine, nor poles (as in subsequent years were erected) to mark, the line of road, so that an hour's continuance of thick drifting snow might totally obliterate, in many places, the distinctions betwixt the highway and the general trackless heath. Hence it happened, that scarcely a winter passed over without yielding the records of perilous or fatal adventures; and, whenever snow-storms abounded, of travellers, more or less in number, perishing by being overwhelmed in the snow-drifts.

It was not long before our traveller, advancing rapidly with vigorous and elastic step within the region of lonesome moorland, became aware that he had entered upon a critical adventure; for having arrived near the sixth milestone on the high-moors over Whitby, he became unexpectedly encircled by a dense and gloomy cloud, attended with a sudden and furious storm of wind and fleecy snow, the snow descending so thick as to envelope him in such dark obscurity, that, for some little time, he could neither see his way to advance nor to return.

Recovering somewhat from his first embarrassment, and considering what might be well to be done, he determined, adventurous as the attempt might be, to go forward toward Salter Gate, yet six miles distant, and not a house on the road. He had made but little progress, however, in advance, before he found he had gone off the turnpike-road; nor did his first attempt, as by a nautical traverse, seem to improve his situation. When brought to a stand in this perplexing condition, it was, that his naturally reflective mind suggested an use of his humble geometrical acquirements, which afforded him essential service. He had observed how the wind first assailed him, with reference to the direction of the line of road, which, fortunately for him, like the roads of ancient construction, generally, followed a steeple-chase directness, regardless of hill or dale, for the point aimed at; and by adjusting his progress on the same angle, in respect to the course of the wind, he hoped to be guided in his now perilous undertaking. "Taking his departure" from this incidental starting-point, he set forward with as much speed as the nature of the ground and the resistance of the storm could well admit, and, proceeding in a straight direction, over hill and dale, through moor and bog, he accomplished another mile, and that so successfully as to reach its termination, to his great satisfaction, scarcely twenty yards from the seventh milestone. Encouraged by this success, he now advanced, in spite of storm and blinding snow-drift, and under painfully reduced strength, approaching at the last very near to exhaustion, until his enterprise and tact were happily rewarded by arriving at Salter Gate, where, in the house for which he originally aimed, he was enabled to obtain both shelter and refreshment. The rest of the enterprise, after encountering various difficulties, from the continuance of the snow on the ground, was in like manner accomplished, so that with no great loss of time he was welcomed in safety at his father's house.

During this arduous and hazardous journey, as his biographer remarks, "he proved the value and accuracy of his geometry whilst traversing the high-moors, the importance of perseverance, and the gracious care of Divine Providence."

SECTION II.—*His first year's Apprenticeship.*

IN the quiet of a country home, my Father now resumed those studies which bore more immediately upon the profession he had chosen, and perseveringly continued them till the time appointed, the middle of March, for his joining his ship. His preparations towards the supplying of his maritime costume and equipment being already made, he repaired to Whitby, and was duly set to work, with others of the destined crew, to rig and fit out the ship. Towards the end of the month the arrangements were so far advanced, that she was hauled down the harbour into a berth convenient for putting to sea. But whilst here a hard gale set in from the north, which brought so heavy a sea into the harbour that the Jane was in danger of breaking adrift. This circumstance called for the prompt and active exertions of the crew to get out cables and hawsers for additional security, an occasion on which my Father received his first lesson on mooring a ship, —a lesson which could not be lost upon one who associated with great physical strength and energy so observant and reflective a mind.

Early in the month of April, the weather proving

favourable whilst the spring-tides prevailed, the Jane put to sea, and for a time made pleasant progress. Nearing the Naze of Norway, however, they were overtaken at night, and that suddenly, by a heavy gale of wind, which in its effect was in no small degree alarming, and from the quality of the crew, indeed, twelve out of about twenty hands being apprentices, some mere lads, and several quite inexperienced, eminently perilous,—for the ship being lightly ballasted, was quickly thrown upon her "beam-ends," the water rising over the lee gunwale till it reached the "combings of the hatches," whilst the requisite measures, demanding instantaneous promptness, were seriously delayed by the general inaptitude of the crew. They were enabled, however, in time to save them from the threatened foundering, to get the sails clewed up, whereon the ship righted, though the sails were left fluttering, the sport and prey of the storm, until the morning. The gale then happily abating, and veering to a favourable quarter, the canvas, as far as preserved to them, which so recently had threatened their destruction, became available for the furtherance of their voyage, and enabled them without further adventure to reach Memel, the port of their destination.

But when outward danger had been safely passed, and nothing but a feeling of perfect security could naturally be realized, the object of this memorial became sensibly alive to the impressiveness of the solemn sentiment of our Church's funeral service—" In the midst of life we are in death!" The ballast had been taken out, and the hold and 'tween-decks cleared to make way for the cargo, when my Father, being below, near a " raft-port,"—an opening at the bow or stern by which a timber cargo is received into the hold,—heard the voice of the Captain calling for a boat's crew to put him on shore. There being no *deck* now laid upon the hold-beams, but only a series of " carlings" from beam to beam, the summons was attempted to be answered by running along these very narrow supports. Ill directed, however, by the very deceptive light admitted by the raft-port, my Father's head came in contact with an unobserved break in the upper deck, by which he was precipitated into the hold, a depth of about twelve feet, and was taken up by his comrades in a state of insensibility. In this alarming condition he remained for several hours, being meanwhile carried for surgical assistance on shore.

He was but barely passed out of the immediate hands of the surgeon, who contemplated his case hopefully, when the carpenter of the Jane was borne to the same place, having also fallen into the hold in a similar way, with an adze in his hand, a fearful cut from which in his forehead added to the severe effects of so considerable a fall.

Under careful and skilful assistance, however, both the endangered sufferers were soon restored, being enabled to return to the ship in about eight days' time,—the carpenter, indeed, with his wound but imperfectly healed, and with a long and conspicuous scar which might have been admonitory for the rest

of his days. The lesson to my Father had not been
forgotten when, near half a century after, on recurring
to the adventure, he remarked, "This was another
kind interposition of Providence which has a claim on
my grateful homage."

Their cargo of timber being completed, they immediately sailed from Memel, and joining convoy at
Elsinore, safely reached the Thames, whither their
cargo was destined.

Whilst the ship was lying at Limehouse, my Father
and another of the apprentices obtained leave, on a
Sunday, to go on shore and visit the great Metropolis,
where they met with another, and to them a previously unknown, species of adventure. On reaching
the city they were accosted by a man dressed in
regimentals (apparently a serjeant), who, pretending
that he was a Yorkshireman and knew them, contrived
to insinuate himself into their confidence, and offered
to guide them in their object of sight-seeing, remarking particularly that they had a fine opportunity of
seeing the King, who was about to attend a general
review in Hyde Park. Catching at a suggestion so
naturally pleasant, they, without an idea of mistrust,
put themselves under his, apparently, friendly guidance, and proceeded in the direction of the Park. On
reaching Temple Bar he invited them to accompany
him into an eating-house, where he ordered refreshments.

But the landlady, on making her appearance—a
respectable and benevolent person, as they subse-

quently had good reason to know—observed and sur-
veyed the little party with a very unusual kind of
scrutiny, first looking the soldier sternly in the face,
and then, with an expression relaxed into compassion,
turned her gaze on his youthful and obviously too
confiding associates. Repeating her scrutiny of their
pretended friend till assured of his identity, she addressed him with an air of stern authority, and commanded him to leave the house. The man affecting
surprise, and 'presuming that she must have mistaken
him,' endeavoured, by a well-practised self-possession,
to avoid the threatened defeat of his insidious purpose. But she, persisting in her knowledge and
accusation of him, and threatening to call in a con-
stable to her aid, succeeded in causing him to feel
that it might be for his safety to take himself off.

On his departure she turned to the wondering young
sailors, and to this effect addressed them:—"I perceive, young men, you are from the country, and are
strangers in London. I am from the country myself,
but I know that man to be a villain. Not long since
he stole some articles from this very house, and I am
fully assured he will wait for you to get you trepanned;
you shall therefore not leave my house this night."

They accordingly remained her guests till the morning, when she allowed them to depart for their ship;
but on offering her compensation for her kindness, she
refused to take anything more than was barely sufficient to pay for their moderate refreshments.

"This act of generous friendship," remarks the

writer of the Memoir, " deserves to be recorded on three accounts: first, for the honour of our common nature ; secondly, to be contrasted with the villany of the pretended soldier; and thirdly, to illustrate the watchful Providence of God."

Having delivered their cargo at Limehouse, and taken in ballast, they sailed on their second voyage, to St. Petersburgh, for a cargo of hemp and iron. Here they were unfortunately caught in the formation of ice, with but little expectation of escaping during the winter. But on the 4th of November, a gale from the eastward having broken up the impeding ice, they immediately sailed, and in four days reached Elsinore, where they expected to join convoy for England. All the men-of-war from home, however, having sailed, they joined a fleet of similarly unprotected ships, num-bering altogether six-and-twenty sail, and together proceeded for England. About half-way across the German ocean, they proved the advantage of their mutual association for defence, a large cutter privateer having hove in sight, and attacked the rear of the fleet. For a considerable time the enemy's fire was directed from a respectful distance against the nearest ships, which they, according to their proportion of armament, as actively returned,—so actively, indeed, that, in their ill-provided warlike stores, they soon expended the greater part of their ammunition. The enemy, however, ignorant of this circumstance, and unable to detach any single vessel, kept aloof, probably for the chance of the night; but the night proved dark, and afforded them a screen from the prowler, and they all escaped unscathed into port.

They reached Portsmouth, their new destination, about the middle of December, and delivered their cargo among the naval stores of the King's Yard.

During the discharging of the cargo, my Father received vexatious abuse, without any provocation on his part, from the chief-mate of the ship, which so annoyed him that, under the impulse of a strongly excited feeling, he had resolved to quit the Jane, and enter on board His Majesty's ship the Royal George, just then passing them from the graving-dock, where she had been undergoing repairs. But reflecting on something which, in the bustle and confusion amongst her crew as she hauled away, he had observed incongruous with his feelings, he happily paused in his hasty resolve, and ultimately decided on submitting himself to a continuance, though under the constant exposure to like arbitrary annoyance, of the duties of his humble station, with a view to the fulfilment of the engagement he had entered into with the owner of the Jane. And, as estimated by the probability of his being involved in the disaster of that ill-fated ship, had he entered on board of her, the decision appeared to be Providentially guided; for at no long interval after this time it was that the Royal George came to her end so strangely, as to place the catastrophe alone and without parallel, amid the varied and marvellous records of our naval history. The story is well known.

She was " careening," for the purpose of having some caulking of her seams effected, or damage of her copper sheathing repaired, whilst anchored at Spithead, with her lower-deck ports open in all imaginable safety. A sudden squall, whilst the ship swung across the tide, laid her on her beam-ends; the water poured in by the open ports in such force and quantity, that she sunk in less than eight minutes, involving officers, men, and visitors, so generally in the common catastrophe, that out of about 1200 souls, or upward, on board, only 331 escaped alive! The brave Admiral Kempenfelt, an experienced and accomplished navigator, who, through many perils of war and tempest had passed unscathed, suffered among the rest, a fate which, very probably, had been that of my Father, had he carried out his impetuously-formed design. But, with the good hand of God upon him, he escaped the then unimagined peril.

On the laying up of the Jane for the winter, the seamen, as usual, were discharged, and the apprentices sent by a coasting vessel passengers to Whitby. My Father repaired to his country home for the interval of service, until summoned again to London, in the early spring of 1781, to join his ship on her being chartered for a voyage to Riga, for a cargo of deals for the Government.

SECTION III.—*His Progress as a Seaman, with Incidents of Sea-Life.*

ENTERING the sea-service as a profession or business, as an unaided adventurer, my Father felt, and ever acted on the feeling, that, under the blessing of Providence, to which he distinctly looked, he must be the fabricator of his own fortune. To learn his profession, from the very elements of a seaman's duty to its most manly and skilful perfection; to acquire a knowledge of navigation, of which he had anticipated but little, and to extend that knowledge to the highest style of seamanship,—constituted the scheme and aspiration of his naturally vigorous and enterprising mind.

But in beginning, as a country lad, at the beginning, with nothing of position, or education, or influence, to raise him above the common and ordinary class of learners in the school of maritime practice, he met with no small difficulty in raising himself, as his purpose was to do, in character and pursuits, above his fellows. His habit was—as soon as raw inexperience enabled him to form a habit—to spend his leisure time, when not on watch, aloof from the galley-congregation of idle, and often profane, companions. And instead of following the useless and time-wasting practices of those around him, his habit was, as opportunity offered, to endeavour, by the help of a few appropriate books, to carry out his former humble acquirements in figures into the really practical "working of a day's work," and "the keeping of the ship's reckoning." Nor, in the ordinary "watch," did he associate intimately with the general body of the crew, preferring, unless he could find a somewhat like-minded aspirant after a better position, to walk alone on the main-deck or forecastle, holding companionship only with his own thoughts.

Two incidents, in connection with this period of my Father's personal history, are fresh in my recollection, —one of them illustrative of his difficult position in refusing familiar association with his fellow mariners; the other illustrative of his success in the acquisition of nautical knowledge, by his own persevering and unaided application.

A marked degree of ill-will, on the part of several of the crew in one of his early voyages, followed his prevailing separation from familiar association with them. This was exhibited by innumerable tokens and expressions, both in word and action. Jeers, insinuations and ridicule, were indulged in with painful and increasing frequency, and these not unmixed with contemptuous or offensive actions. Naturally spirited and quick-tempered, as the subject of this ungenerous behaviour was constitutionally, it was hard to restrain the expression of indignation, or to resist the urgent impulse to a just retaliation. But, acting on the system of non-retaliation, so long as they kept "hands off," he bore this persecution with extraordinary forbearance. For constitutionally strong and energetic, few would have been able to compete with him, as the issue proved, if the lion in him were roused. His height was now near six feet; his frame was strong-boned and muscular; his vigour and activity were unusually great. But he restrained himself to the utmost, and his great strength, as to the perceptions of his associates, continued long unknown.

At length the time of resistance, which he could not but feel must some time or other arrive, came. It happened in this way. My Father had descended the deck after his watch, and with the view, I believe, of retiring, as usual, to a quiet part of the vessel alone, when two of the crew made on him a premeditated attack—a kind of half-joking assault by no trifling hits, rudely grasping him at the same moment, one on each side. Endeavouring to shake them off without coming to extremities, he quietly requested them to desist. Their sinister defiance and rudeness in grappling him increased in offensiveness. "You had *better* be quiet;" "Do be quiet;" "Let me alone;" and other peace-desiring solicitations of like kind, were tried. But the attack and effort to throw him became more determined. At length, after a firm and decided utterance to the command "Hands off!" indicating that the spirit was up, the attacked party in his turn grappled the necks of his assailants, one with each hand, and, taking advantage of the muscular reaction, after they had made a simultaneous but ineffective thrust against him, he flung them, by a Samson-like impulse, right and left, and both of them fell, heavily, prostrate on the deck! So unawares was the throw, and so totally unsustained by cautionary preparation, that, as to one of them, the subject of this self-earned retribution, lay motionless, insensible, and bleeding! Others of the crew who had noticed the scuffle came up, and seeing the man lie so helpless, and apparently inanimate, exclaimed, " He is dead! Scoresby has done for him!" Happily, the catastrophe was not so serious. By and by there was a return of motion, and obvious reflux of life; but when at length the prostrate had, with much difficulty, gathered himself up, he contrived to stagger meekly enough away, without noticing the author of his humiliation, or ever after attempting either a renewal of his bravadoes, or a retaliation for his severe punishment.

It is hardly needful to say that, from that time, my Father was allowed to pursue his own way without further molestation or offensive remark; and that the respect which seamen are generally ready to yield to true bravery and superior skill was as generously be-stowed by the right-minded of the crew, at least, as the fine and successful effort of the unfairly assaulted one deserved.

The other incident was of a totally different cha-racter.

My Father had early discovered, on his studying out the rules and practice of navigation, as set forth in the comparatively humble nautical works of that period, that there was much that was gratuitous, or arbitrary and uncertain, in the allowances and correc-tions proposed to be made on the "ship's log." On these things he made his own observations, and, in calculating the ship's position, which he was now tolerably well able to accomplish, he made his *own corrections*, instead of those marked on the "log-board" by the officer of the watch. His position, in consequence, often differed very materially from the ordinary reckoning, as well as from that kept by one of his associates among the apprentices, who, like himself, was anxious for advancement in his profession.

At the time referred to he was in progress of his third voyage in the Jane, when, having taken in their cargo of spars for masts, at Riga, they were on their return towards Elsinore.

On the third day after their departure from Riga, a little after twelve at noon,—the wind being easterly and the weather foggy, and the ship under studding-sails, making a progress of about five knots,—the two young navigators finished the day's reckoning, and then proceeded to compare the results. The position of the ship, as calculated simply from the register on the log-board, necessarily differed from that deduced from the same data on which the judgment had been exercised, and various allowances and alterations made. Observing the nature of the difference, which amounted to several miles, the intelligent youth exclaimed, " Why, by your account, we are just running down Bornholm; but my journal is the same as the ship's, and we are going round to the northward of the island." The question being discussed with considerable animation betwixt them, it excited observation

among the crew, and reached the ears of the Captain.
A sharp look-out for land was ordered, when, in
brief space, the look-out on the forecastle shouted
"Breakers a-head!" "Put down the helm—Let go the
anchor!" cried the Captain. The manœuvre was just
in time to save the ship from destruction. When she
swung to her anchor it was in four-and-a-half fathoms
water; the breakers were close by the stern, and the
stern not above twenty fathoms from the shore,—and
the shore, as had been predicted, was that of the
island of Bornholm!

The weather soon cleared up, when they found
themselves in a sandy bay on the south-east side of
the island. The sea not being considerable they soon
got under weigh, and sailing round the island to the
southward, they reached Elsinore the next day. "It
was to this private reckoning kept by Mr. Scoresby,"
observes the writer of the Memoir of which I have
here and elsewhere availed myself, "and the debate
to which it led, that the preservation of the ship and
cargo may evidently be ascribed."

" The reward which Mr. Scoresby received for this
piece of essential service was such," adds the biographer, "as the deserving too frequently obtain from
their superiors in office, who feel themselves insulted
when their deficiencies are exposed by the efforts of
their superiors in merit. The preservation of the ship
and cargo," by the superiority of a mere tyro in seamanship—a young apprentice, "drew upon him, especially, the envy of the mate, who, it will be remem-

bered, had aforetime shown a painful measure of ill-will, and the disapprobation of some of the inferior officers. These ungenerous influences, in their combined effect, rendered his situation so uncomfortable that, on reaching the Thames, he left the ship, and engaged in an Ordnance-armed storeship, the Speedwell cutter, destined to carry out stores to Gibraltar."

This step, which it is to be apprehended had not the sanction of the parties to whom he was apprenticed, was attended with consequences which, with one whose mind was early directed to regard a Providential hand perpetually engaged in guiding, controlling, or, for merciful ends, rebuking the affairs of man, could hardly fail to be impressive, and to yield salutary convictions of the error into which a manly indignation at ungenerous usage and jealous antipathy had urged him.

SECTION IV.—*Capture by the Enemy, and Escape from a Spanish Prison.*

THE Speedwell was soon equipped, and, the service being urgent,—the relief of the garrison at Gibraltar,—with all haste got to sea. But admirably as this fast-sailing cutter was adapted for a service requiring all possible despatch, the weather proved very unfavourable for making a satisfactory, much less a rapid, progress.

The delay was additionally trying to those on board the cutter, from the deprivations in which the unexpected length of the voyage, by reason of calms and adverse winds, involved them.   For, economical of room for the requisite stores whilst on the passage to the Straits, the Speedwell was sent out so inadequately supplied with water, that the crew were reduced to a distressingly short allowance.

This incident, however, afforded occasion and opportunity for the development of my Father's peculiar acuteness of intellect, and the exercise of his natural science.   Whilst suffering greatly from thirst, the idea occurred to him that some refreshment might possibly be derived through the medium of the pores of the skin by bathing—an idea which the calmness of the weather enabled him to put to the test and satisfactorily to verify.   For on undressing and taking a rope for his security, and jumping overboard, he realized, even beyond his expectations, a decidedly refreshing influence—such as, under his report, to induce most of the officers and crew not only to try the same experiment, but to render it a prevailing practice, whenever the state of the weather would permit.

But a new incident soon substituted for this another species of deprivation and suffering.   They had advanced within sight of the Spanish coast, when, on the 26th of October 1781, being off Cape Trafalgar, they fell in with a force so overwhelmingly superior, as to render resistance useless.   The cutter became a prize to the enemy, and my Father, with his associates, prisoners of war.   They were taken into Cadiz

Bay, and he, with some others, were marched into
the interior of the country, to St. Lucar la Major,
a small town of Andalusia, seated on the river
Guadiana, a tributary of the Quadalquiver.

Here, they were not ungenerously treated; whilst
the rigour of imprisonment, as at first practised, became gradually relaxed under the imagined security
of the captives. The degree of liberty, indeed, after
awhile became such, that the prisoners were entrusted
to go unguarded, to some distance from their quarters,
to fetch water. In this indulgence my Father saw
a chance of escape, which, being participated in by
one of his associates, a spirited young sailor and
friend, they privately conferred thereon, and ultimately arranged to encounter the difficulties and
risks of the adventure.

Availing themselves of an occasion when various
circumstances gave favour to the experiment, they
proceeded, in their usual manner, to the place where
water was procured; and, finding themselves unobserved, they walked away, as if incidently strolling
about, until they had obtained shelter, I believe,
from a wood. Here they pushed rapidly on, dropping
their water-vessels in a place of concealment, until
having made what they deemed a sufficient progress
to baffle an ordinary pursuit, they hid themselves for
the remainder of the day. Then, with the stars only
for their guidance, they travelled, as by a steeple-
chase route, throughout the night towards the coast.
This, indeed, became their prevalent plan of pro-

ceeding, to rest in some concealment by day, and to travel by night.

Their progress proved, indeed, fully as adventurous, consistently with their safety, as the liveliest imagination could have pictured. The perils and difficulties they encountered from native Spaniards, or from the pursuit of troops sent after them; from their imperfect concealment during the day, or critical exposure in their progress during the night; from the applications which they were necessitated to make on the *generosity* of the enemies of their country for relief and sustenance,—for they had been deprived of everything they possessed except two little bundles of clothing which, in contemplation of the adventure, they had previously concealed beyond their prison; from their suspicious appearance in the dress, and with the language of foreigners, inducing attempts to give them up to the public authorities; with the aid and consolations, on the other hand, which they occasionally met with from the sympathies of the gentler sex, even whilst others were seeking their recapture,—yielded altogether a series of exciting and anxious incidents, which, if the particulars could be thoroughly recalled, might afford materials for a history of really romantic interest. The fact of kind and generous sympathy, and effective aid from women, I well remember as constituting a touching element in the relation of their perilous undertaking.   As Mungo Park, in his varied and perilous travels, ever found kindness, in the instinct of a sympathising nature, from women, savage though their race might be, so did my Father and his associate realize, among the Spanish peasants, the like experience. Once, in particular, I remember its being stated, that when our adventurers had confided themselves to the supposed friendly shelter of a cottage, the master of the cottage stepped away, in order to give information about the fugitives at some neighbouring magisterial or military post, whilst his wife, compassionating the proscribed strangers in a foreign land, meanwhile contrived to give them a secret warning of their peril, and at the same time to provide the means, by the back of the cottage, for their prompt and effectual escape.

The remainder of the story, so far as relates to their escape from the Spanish shores, may be summarily given.

Under the guidance of a gracious and prospering Providence, they arrived safely at the coast, and, happily, when circumstances proved singularly favourable for the completion of their adventurous project. For it so happened (and happened it not by the providential ordering of times and circumstances to fit each other for an issue accordant with confiding trust and fervent prayers?) that when they reached this most critical position, they found a *cartel*—an English vessel which had disembarked her freight of prisoners of war, brought out in exchange—just preparing to depart for the land of their hopes!

Penniless and friendless, as our now reanimated adventurers were, besides being specially exposed to detection on the well-watched shores of an enemy's country, it required no little management and tact to get off during the night; that so, fugitives as they were on the one part, and intruders on the other, they might elude the observation both of the Spanish officers and the captain of the cartel. But the same gracious furtherance, as heretofore they had experienced, continued to prosper their way, and all difficulties and hazards were safely accomplished; and, by the friendly aid of the crew, upon whose humanity they cast themselves, the means of concealment were provided until the circumstances of present risk and anxiety should have passed away.

SECTION V.—*Rewards of Masterly Seamanship.*

WE are here brought to the describing of an incident particularly characteristic of my Father's talent as an accomplished practical seaman.

After the vessel was fairly at sea, and, furthered by a favourable wind, in encouraging progress on her way to England, my Father and his gallant associate ventured to appear upon deck. The natural surprise of the Captain, on finding two intruding auxiliaries amongst his people, assumed no very friendly character, even when the daring and almost romantic undertaking of the strangers had been made known to him. On the contrary, he received their explanation with no small measure of anger, and followed up his pitiless inconsideration with heartless threatenings.

He threatened, with much apparent determination, either to land them again amongst their enemies, or give them up as a boon, though of most unwilling hands, to some English ship-of-war. Their appeals to his sympathy and benevolence were unavailing. Their offer "to work their passage," which *they* thought might be a compensation for their provision, was slighted, on the ground that "the crew was sufficient." But at length the Captain suggested the alternative, at which he evidently aimed, of their paying for their accommodation and passage to England. Being, as we have shown, absolutely penniless, this was a difficult requirement, though the Captain got over it by proposing that they should sign a document pledging themselves, on arrival in England, to a payment which they deemed most exorbitant. With this demand the urgency of their own purpose, and the fear of the threatenings of the Captain, obliged them to comply, and the paper was drawn up and signed.

Fortunately for them, the Bay of Biscay maintained its too dreaded celebrity at the season referred to, by becoming the scene of a formidable sea and storm. The gale commenced rather suddenly, and became rapidly so fierce, that the seamen, who were quite inadequate in number, as well as in capabilities, were unable to get in the sail within the limits of safety. The canvas was flapping furiously aloft, and all efforts to reef were distressingly slow. Meanwhile my Father and his comrade were eyed with indignation and surprise by the Captain, as they moved on the deck, or stood holding by the "weather-rail," with quiet composure, as if ignorant of, or indifferent to, the increasing peril of the position of the ship. At last, an exclamation of astonishment burst from the Captain, that, regardless of the general safety, they should not offer a helping hand. They replied most coolly, "that the crew, they understood, was ample, and needed no help of theirs, and they were but passengers!" The perplexed commander turned away in ill-concealed vexation. Still the gale increased in severity, till the ship was thrown almost on her "beam-ends," and their situation became quite alarming. He then renewed his application under a severe taunt, as if it were unmanly to allow the crew to struggle so against the difficulties of the storm, and they, two able and efficient seamen, looking on! "Destroy the paper," they said, "and let us work our passage, and we shall be ready for your orders." Desperate now, in his anxiety to save the canvas and spars, and, indeed, to secure the safety of the ship, the Captain produced the important and vexatious paper, and tearing it passionately into pieces, he scattered its fragments on the wild waste of waters to leeward.

Forthwith the two emancipated passengers spring forward to their duty as members of the crew. They could not have been unobservant of the slovenly manner in which yards and sails had been prepared for the operation of reefing,—so ill-arranged, indeed, with a ship heeling almost yard-arm in the water, and sails

c 2

flying over the yards to leeward, as to render the
operation scarcely practicable. First of all the yards
are, in a seamanlike manner, laid to pass; braces are
hauled taught, and lower yards steadied by the
" trusses " and " lifts;" " reef-tackles," with a helping
hand probably by the men aloft, are well hauled out,
and the inflated and flapping canvas pressed in by the
"buntlines" to the yards,—and then, bounding into
the rigging, their feet scarcely touch the "ratlines," as,
aided by the elasticity of tension in the shrouds, they
ascend up the mast. Way is instinctively made by
the previously dispirited hands for my Father to the
" weather-earing " of the topsail, and for his friend to
leeward. Here, as in most other operations, his singular energy, strength and skill, render him wonderfully efficient. Seated across the yard-arm, with
shoulder steadied and supported by the " lift,"—the
" earing" passed round and reeved in the "reef-cringle"
of the sail,—he is enabled, with little aid from the hands
on the yard, to haul out the sail by vast muscular
strength, skilfully applied, to the fitting position, when
the cry " Haul out to leeward," is replied to by
his associate there with similar vigour and celerity of
action, so that the enclosed section of the sail, previously so intractable under other hands, is in a few
moments laid compact on the yard, and securely en-
folded within the "reef-points." Thus reef succeeded
reef, till the broad flapping sail displayed but its
smallest dimensions—the "close-reef" adapted for the
storm, whilst corresponding operations were performed

on the other sails with marvellous smartness and
despatch ; for the superior energy and commanding
efficiency of these leaders, of a previously heartless
and dispirited crew, had happily infused into all a new
spirit of confidence, and stimulated to unwonted effort
to imitate their admired ability, and thus to become
useful helps in the task to be accomplished.

Within a less interval of time, perhaps, than had
previously been wasted in inefficient endeavours to
accomplish the duties required by the sudden violence
of the storm, topsails are reefed and set compactly to
the wind ; courses and other sails are reefed or made
snug by handing ; top-gallant-yards, with spars and
flying gear aloft, are sent down upon deck ; and the
ship, now no longer pressed down by overwhelming
top-weight and fluttering sails, is restored to the desired equilibrium, and snugly prepared to encounter
and weather the storm !

From this time the duty of the ship was well and
smartly done. The superiority of my Father as a
thorough practical seaman must have been both felt
and acknowledged : the distance at which he soared
beyond the others was too great and obvious for the
intrusion even of that bane of social concord—jealousy;
and the effect seems to have been the infusion of a
higher character into the ordinary crew. Well,
therefore, did our fugitives from a Spanish prison
repay to ship, captain, owners and crew, the benefits
they themselves received.

SECTION VI.—*Entrance on, and Progress in training
in, the Greenland Whale-Fishery.*

AFTER his exciting adventure in escaping from
imprisonment in an enemy's country, my father retired, for a season, from his seafaring pursuits. He
returned to the homestead of his fathers, where, as-
sisting in the management of the farm, he remained
about two or three years. During this interval he
married; the object of his choice being Lady Mary,
(viz. Mary, with the prefix of Lady, taken, not osten-
tatiously, but in rural simplicity, from the characteristic designation of the day of her birth, which
was on *Lady-day*), the eldest daughter of Mr. John
Smith, of Cropton,—a rural district about five-and-
twenty miles from Whitby,—who resided on a small
landed property which he had inherited from his
ancestors.

By no means satisfied, however, with this retirement,—which recent hard and perilous service had,
for a time, rendered congenial to his feelings,— and
as little contented with the limitation of his unusual
energies to such a contracted scope of employment,
he turned his attention again to the sea. And in this
object he at length found a congenial opening, in a
region and employment admirably adapted to his physical constitution and adventurous spirit, the *Greenland Whale Fishery;* a trade which, at this period,
the latter end of the eighteenth century, was pursued
with considerable enterprise from the port of Whitby.

On this new species of maritime service he embarked in the ship Henrietta, Captain Crispin Bean,
in the spring of the year 1785, as one of the seamen.
Of the incidents of his training in this adventurous
and stirring profession, we have, unfortunately, no
special records. To the requirements, however, in
every species of knowledge and duty connected with
the Arctic navigation and the capture of the huge
cetacea of the north, he gave himself with such tact
and perseverance, that, on his sixth voyage, we find
him to have risen over the heads of all his original
associates, and occupying the position of second
officer, the *specksioneer* of the ship.*

A single incident, though of the most trifling
nature, has been preserved in connection with this
period of my Father's life, which I am induced to
record, simply because there was something in it
illustrative of character.

As the ships employed in the whale fishery in
the spring and summer were usually *laid up* during
the rest of the year, it was the frequent practice of
the officers, who were generally engaged from year
to year, to embark as seamen in the coasting trade
during the interval of winter. My Father, habitually
energetic and industrious, and having now an increasing family to support, adopted this commendable
course. On one occasion it so happened that he was

* The title "specksioneer," derived from the Dutch, is applied to
the officer who has special charge of the fishing apparatus, and the conduct of the flensing operations in the fishery. He is also a principal
harpooner.

employed in a vessel whose chief officer, the mate, was a young man possessing a full share of self-conceit, evinced by a not unfrequent exhibition of supercilious assumption of superiority—characteristics excessively obnoxious to my Father's manly disposition. But, notwithstanding the occasional exhibition of an offensive manner towards himself as well as others, such was always his high sense of the *duty of obedience to superiors,* and of the importance, in principle, of *proper subordination,* that he bore with restrained feelings in silence this youthful and vexatious folly. An occasion, however, occurred, in which he might legitimately suffer the fault to chastise itself, and it is to that to which my story refers.

The vessel was lying in port about to take in ballast. In this operation, which is often effected (as in this case) by the shovel of "ballast-heavers" out of loaded "lighters" laid alongside the ship, there is a liability to scatter a good deal of the shingle or other material, so as to fall overboard to the encumbrance of the harbour. To prevent this damage to the navigation, it is in many places a harbour regulation that a canvas screen or sail, called a "port-sail," should be placed below the small port-hole cut in the side of the ship for the reception of ballast, so as to catch the ballast-heavers' scatterings.

In the good ship, the ——, however, this canvas protector happened to be wanting when ballast was about to be taken in. The mate, with a manner (it is presumed) of excessive superciliousness, came to

my Father with a "*bolt*" (or roll) of canvas, asking
him, as if doubting his capacity, whether he could
make such a thing ? and then requesting him to set
immediately to work to supply the lack of port-sails.
Assuming a look of meekest simplicity, which for
such a just retribution my Father could well put on,
he quietly asked, in reference to the order to make
port-sails, " how *many* he was to make ? " Mistaking
the look of simplicity for simpleness itself, the young
officer, as he turned jeeringly away, replied, " *half-
a-dozen*, to be sure."

One only, or two, at the most, could possibly be
required ; but, to punish arrogancy, the order was
strictly regarded. Some hours subsequently the
mate returned to the place where the work of the
sail-needle was being actively carried on, when, to
his astonishment and vexation, he found the deck
covered with the breadths of canvas *cut out* for the
half-dozen port-sails, and some two or three of them
already seamed together ! His fierce demand, " Why
have you cut up the whole bolt of canvas ? " was
responded to in the former quiet manner of simplicity, " Did you not order me to make half-a-
dozen ? "

Whilst thus justly chastised for his own folly, and
biting his lips with vexation,—the vexation being
the more exciting because *consciously self-earned*,—
he could not refrain from resorting to abuse, where
reason and justice must fail him. But singularly
enough it happened, whilst the altercation which

ensued was being carried on, and when it had been broadly intimated to him, I believe, that his further services could be well dispensed with, that a letter, just then brought by some one coming on board, was put into my Father's hand, offering him the unexpected appointment and preferment which constitute the subject of our next chapter. He was thus enabled, with no small advantage of position over the still fretted and abusive officer, to say, " If you are not satisfied with what I have commenced, I can leave you to do it yourself."

In concluding this chapter, it comes appropriately in connection, to mention something of the state of my Father's mind and feelings with respect to the grand object of this probationary state with man—the attainment and furtherance of a religious life.

On this topic I am the better enabled to write satisfactorily, because of the repeated references to it which I have heard my Father make in after-life. At all times, within my own recollection, he evinced a very marked regard for religion, with a clear apprehension of the great principles of our holy faith, and an ardent desire for the experience of its divine consolations. But he used to refer back, with a kind of longing regret, to the days of his youth, when he had *felt* the consolations of godliness, and realized the happiness of heavenly meditations. Often (as I have heard him intimate) whilst pursuing his agricultural labours, and not unfrequently, too, when walking to and fro in his night-watch at sea,—he had been privileged to realize that enviable feeling of peaceful happiness, in the lifting up of the heart in pious meditations and communings heavenward, which constitutes at once an experimental evidence and present reward of the reception of the Gospel of our Lord and Saviour Jesus Christ. For, however it may fall short in the ardency of its perceptions, or however it may be liable to be confounded with the hasty and transient impulses of mere excitement, yet, in its nature, and according to its degree, the feeling thus realized belongs, I doubt not, to that truly enviable class of Christian experiences described by St. Paul, as " the peace of God, which passeth all understanding," and as the rejoicing " with joy unspeakable and full of glory."

Chapter II.

HIS COMMENCEMENT AND PROGRESS IN WHALE-FISHING ENTERPRISE, AS A COMMANDER.

Section I.—*Disappointment in his first Command.*

In the history of men who, relatively to their prospects by birth, have attained to distinction in life, there will generally be found some special incident, sometimes apparently trifling in itself, or some particular circumstance, or chain of circumstances, in their professional career, on which, under Providence, their fortune manifestly turned.

Both the incident and the circumstance referred to were clearly and strikingly marked in my Father's history. The *incident* appears in what occasioned the disgust which he took in early life at farming occupations, whereby he was stimulated to enter upon a sea-faring life. The *circumstance*, or chain of circumstances, we find in the important preferment which unexpectedly, as to the occasion, was given to him when, over the heads of many associates, he was appointed to his first command.

Crispin Bean, the captain under whom my Father had had his training and experience in Arctic adventure, was, for *his time*, a successful whale-fisher. For,

in the course of from seventeen to twenty years in
which he followed this commerce, he realized a *small*
fortune, sufficient, at least, with a little patrimony, to
satisfy his very moderate desires and requirements, and
to induce him to retire, whilst in fulness of vigour, from
his arduous profession. He was a man of excellent
character, and one for whom my Father always retained a sincere regard, and towards whom he was
ever ready to show kindly consideration, when his
means for subsistence and comfort were less sufficient
in after-life. A vivid remembrance of Mr. Bean's
regard and preference for him, on the turning point
of his temporal destiny, was observably retained, and
was elicited, as I had myself not unfrequent opportunities of noticing, both in his manner of speaking of
his former commander, and in his readiness to minister
to him in acts of kindness.

It was after his voyage in the year 1790, that Mr.
Bean announced to his owner, Nicholas Piper, Esq.,
of Pickering, his intention of relinquishing his command, and retiring from the sea. Himself entirely
unprepared for appointing a successor, Mr. Piper
enquired whether there was any one, among the
officers of the Henrietta, whom he (Mr. Bean) could
recommend for a Master? Mr. Bean, well observant
of my Father's persevering energy, seaman-like
talent, and general superiority, replied,—" There is
Scoresby, the specksioneer, who, I think, is the man
for the duty." And to him, with but little delay in
further investigation, the command, to the agreeable

surprise of my Father, and the jealous vexation of some of his brother officers, was transferred.

Mr. Piper, however, whilst so promptly exercising this generous confidence in his appointment, failed, in consistency, when proceeding with the measures for carrying it into effect. Considering his limited measure of experience, when contrasted with the much longer engagement in the fishery of the then chief officer, and some of the leading harponeers, he, unfortunately, took *upon himself* to re-engage these men for the ensuing voyage,—a proceeding which, however prudential, my Father felt to be at once uncourteous and unwise, though a measure which he was by no means in a position either to contravene or satisfactorily to resist. Every ground of hope, however, which he might have indulged in respect to any favourable views of such a principle, in its working, failed, whilst his very worst apprehensions were more than realized.

This result, indeed, came out the more characteristically, because of the singular unfavourableness of the season, wherein he made his first trial, for the objects of the adventure. The fishery, in general, proved unprecedentedly unsuccessful. Of seven ships which set out from Whitby, (the port from whence the Henrietta sailed,) one, the Marlborough, was lost; four returned " clean,"—that is, without any cargo ; and two had but one fish each—one of them very small. Tradition has it—and the tradition I can well believe to be a historical fact—that the cargoes of the whole Whitby fleet of *Greenland* whalers (except one) from the fishery of 1791, were carried overland to Pickering, a distance of 21 miles, in one wagon!

It was in the worst class, that of "clean ships," in which the Henrietta stood at the conclusion of this unpropitious season. But she so stood, not by any means deservedly, as regarded either the talent and perseverance of her new Captain, or the opportunities which his enterprise had afforded to his officers and crew for a position of, at least, leading prosperity. My Father, indeed, whilst often speaking in after-times of this trying, mortifying, and, as to his prospects in life, perilous failure, was known to remark, that such were the opportunities which his own people had, of doing as well as the most successful of his competitors, that there was scarcely a "fish" caught by the whole Greenland fleet, but whilst the Henrietta was in company, or during the capture of which he was not within view!

It was not the wish of the leading officers of the Henrietta, however, that their position should be different. A strong feeling of jealousy was injuriously cherished by certain officers over whom my Father had been preferred; and so far was this carried, and so variously indicated, that it became evident that their wish and *design* was, *that their commander should be found in the most humiliating position* amongst his fellow fishermen. The reality of the existence of this feeling was manifested in various ways. Among the early indications of a conspiracy which my Father clearly detected, was the positive and wilful inattention of some principal officers to the objects of their enterprise, when he was in bed, with the substitution of idle, if not venomous, converse, for officer-like diligence and watchfulness. For on one occasion, when being on very promising fishing-ground, he had sent a boat " on bran,"—the term used for designating the condition of a whale-boat when stationed afloat, with the crew ready for instant action, watching for the incidental appearance of a whale,—he heard, whilst lying anxiously awake in his bed, the subdued creaking of the "tackles," as of a cautious and surreptitious hoisting up of the boat ; and, on afterwards going unexpectedly on deck, he found the "watch," both officers and men, engaged as we have just stated.

Attempts on the part of the officers to direct or dictate, not unfrequently made, failed, as was right they should do, except in one instance (judging from the case being often alluded to by my Father with regret), where the yielding to a proposition against his better judgment met with its consistent rebuke. A number of whales had been fallen in with, and the greater part of the boats had been sent out in pur-suit. Reckless and ill-conditioned they pulled about hither and thither, frightening many, but harpooning none, of the objects of chase. For a considerable period the same folly or inefficiency was being enacted, and yet " fish" in encouraging numbers were still to be seen. The chief mate, one Matthew

Smith, came to my Father to remonstrate with him
for keeping the boats so long abroad without something to exhilarate the men,—urging, that spirits, as
he said was usual, should be sent to them, or it could
not be expected that they could either succeed or
persevere. Though more than doubtful of the wisdom of employing stimulants in an adventure requiring the greatest coolness and self-possession, my
Father unfortunately yielded, and ordered the steward
to supply a quantity of brandy for being carried out
to the absent sailors. But the mate's boat, which
was sent with this *refreshment* (?) was seen, after it
had proceeded a mile or so from the ship, to cease
rowing, and "lie to on its oars;" and there, as my
Father's sure telescope told him, they remained, till
the crew had " drank themselves drunk." Then, in
their mad folly, they proceeded to the field of fishing
enterprise, and effectually marred any chance of success, if a single honest harpooner were there, and
gave a new and additional impulse to the existing
recklessness and disaffection.

But private resistance of orders, as well as apparent
neglect of opportunities frequently afforded them of
advancing the grand object of the voyage, ultimately
grew into the most aggravated form of insubordina-
tion—*mutiny*.

On one occasion, when the Henrietta had been
pushed into an unwonted position of imagined peril
among the ice by her commander's adventurous spirit,
the alarm of her crew urged their disaffection into

open mutiny. They gathered themselves together, and proceeded to the quarter-deck, to demand (as I have understood the incident) their being released from so perilous a situation. My Father's disregard of their remonstrances, and expressed determination to persevere, were at length met by brute force and open violence. One of the men, excited by his companions' clamours, and his own dastardly rage, seized a hand-spike, and aimed a desperate blow, which might have been fatal, on the head of his Captain. But, now roused to the exertion of his heretofore unimagined strength and tact, he, whilst warding the blow with his hand, disarmed the assailant, and seizing him, as I have been told, in his athletic arms, actually flung him headlong among his associates, like a quoit from the hands of the player, filling the whole party with amazement at his strength and power, and for the moment arresting, under the influence of the feeling, the unmanly pursuance of their mutinous purposes.

The power of one against so many who had committed themselves to a penal act and assault, however, not being likely to continue to avail him, my Father, with a decision of purpose scarcely less surprising than his power of action, ordered a boy to take the helm, and whilst himself and others, whom his example might influence, " squared the yards," directed the ship's course (the wind being fair) *homeward*. Their demand to be released from the ice being thus yielded, and, with circumstances so very different from what they had expected, reduced,

for a while, both the mutinous and insubordinate of
the crew, to a sort of dogged quiescence. But when
the ship, having cleared the ice, was still kept on the
same course, and when ice and haunts of whales began
to be left far astern, anxiety and alarm took place in
the breasts of the authors of the mischief, who now,
in their turn, felt just cause for dreading the issue
of a proceeding which they had thus unexpectedly
provoked. Words of unwonted calmness were now
dropped by one or other of the officers, in hopes of
eliciting some indication that the homeward direction
was but a threat. Hints of the loss to the owners and
himself were thrown out, if he followed out his apparent purpose ; but all to no purpose—the Henrietta
still wended her way before the home-blowing breeze
with steady and unrestrained progress. At length,
so great was the alarm excited, that the bold and
blustering mutineers became subdued, and they came
forward, backed by their subordinates in the crew,
humbly soliciting that the ship might be hauled on a
wind again for Greenland, and promising that themselves, and every man aboard, would submit to orders,
and do their utmost to further the object on which
they had embarked.

To have persisted in a purpose undertaken from
necessity, the result of which could only be of unmixed injury to his employers as well as himself, when
yet there was a chance, however faint, of doing something in respect to the intention of the adventure,
might have been deemed an act of obstinacy, rather

than wisdom. Not, therefore, to lose any chance of
success, which this demonstration of better feeling
might seem to promise, the ship was forthwith hauled
to the wind, and, as circumstances of wind and
weather allowed, every effort of seamanship was
employed for hastening their return to the fishing-
ground northward. The sunshine, however, which
had rendered the gathering in of a limited harvest
possible, was now departed, and all subsequent endeavours to make up for lost time and opportunities
proved fruitless, so that the talented and efficient
commander of the Henrietta had the mortification
of reporting the result of his first and trial adventure
as "a clean ship!"

On their arrival in port, the designs of the dis-
affected became gradually developed. It was hoped,
and evidently expected, that my Father, failing of
success, would be superseded; and it ultimately came
out, though not until the whole scheme of this nefa-
rious conspiracy had been enacted, and the failure of
the experiment determined, that it had been matter
of promise or arrangement, in the event of the chief
officer obtaining the command, that the other officers
in succeeding ranks should have a step in the way of
promotion; and that the men, generally, should have
better, and more *equal* treatment, and, as they were
vainly flattered, be rewarded with higher wages!

Indications of this dastardly attempt to arrest the
advancement of a young and enterprising commander
appeared in two or three circumstances, which oc-

curred soon after the Henrietta's return to Whitby. One of these was the discovery of a letter, fastened conspicuously on one of the sails, addressed to Mr. Bean, the former captain, "requesting him to procure another master, Captain Scoresby having left the vessel, or gone ashore."

Another circumstance, of a bolder character, I remember being related, which, however, operated in a manner directly the reverse of what was designed by the originators of the ungenerous device. A party of the officers, three or four in number, proceeded to the owner's residence—I believe over the Moors to Pickering—for the express purpose of complaining of my Father's unfitness for the command. One of their reasons, more curious than manly, was founded on observation of their commander's *fearless and adventurous practice, as a navigator,*—entirely different from the habit of the times. The complaint was to the effect, " that, instead of keeping the ship clear of danger in the fishery, he was continually running them into the ice; and his daringness was such that, if he should be continued in the command, *he would lose the ship and drown them all!* "

On a sensible man like Mr. Piper, the information, as to enterprising character, conveyed by objections of this kind, was by no means lost. His reflection thereon, as I understood it to have been, was, " Why this is the very sort of man we need!"

My Father was not, of course, without his anxieties as to what the issue might be. He had embarked in a post of great responsibility, where, beyond the ordinary qualifications of the navigator, *success as a fisherman* was looked for, and so prominently regarded, too, that successfulness, above all other qualities, stood absorbingly pre-eminent. Having failed on his first, and most critical, trial, he anxiously expressed his regrets at his failure, when he first met his disappointed and suffering owner. But he, having meanwhile, I believe, spoken on the subject to his former captain (Mr. Bean), replied encouragingly, "It can't be helped: you must try again." The confiding owner, however, could not but be a little surprised when, on the first fitting occasion after the intimation of his re-appointment, my Father, meekly, but firmly, informed him, "that if he again took the command he must have the appointment of all the hands—both officers and general crew." Mr. Piper's usual "Pooh! pooh!" at a demand so unexpected, produced no change in the reasonable requirements of his anxious, but decided dependent. He consulted Mr. Bean thereon, and he, it is reported, recommended acquiescence on the part of the owner. At all events the owner did acquiesce. The happy effect and result will appear in our next section.

SECTION II.—*His Second Adventure, and commencing Prosperity.*

UNDER the fitting authority yielded to my Father, in respect to the absolute selection and engagement of his officers and crew, he acted with equal wisdom and decision. His first act was to discharge the whole of his old and self-assumed accomplished or experienced officers, and to replace them with younger and more tractable men; some of those who had served with him in his first command, whose characters he had appreciated, being advanced from inferior stations to places of responsibility.

The principle that had been conceded by the owner to his captain, as to the absolute selection of his crew, was, however, in a very minor appointment, attempted to be interfered with; but it only served to bring out in greater distinctiveness the character with whom he had to deal. The circumstance was this:—On the fitting out of the ship in the spring of 1792, my Father, on going on board one morning for his usual superintendence of the work, observed a stranger,— one whom he had not himself engaged,—busily employed, as if quite installed in office, about the cooking department. In surprise he asked the would-be *cook* "who had sent him there?" "The owner," he replied, "had *shipped* him as the cook."

Without a word further, and without regarding consequences, so momentous to himself which might result, he gave himself up to the manly impulse of his mind, determining either to have the appointment revoked, or to relinquish a post which had formed at once the object of his aspirings and the summit of his hopes. His manner on the occasion, whilst most respectful to his superior, was as unequivocally firm, as his mind was decided. Taking the "ship's papers" from their safe custody in a compartment of the cabin, viz. the ship's register, certain bonds claimed by the Customs and Excise, and other documents required to be held by the ship's commander,—he proceeded immediately on shore to Mr. Piper's apartments, at once presenting them, and in so doing, resigning his command into the hands of the astonished owner. His astonishment was hardly lessened when, on being asked the reason of this strange conduct, my Father referred him to the appointment, without his personal sanction, of a cook to the ship. The remonstrative "pooh! pooh! pooh!" proved of no more avail than on a former occasion; but Mr. Piper's naturally good sense prevailing over his mortified pride of authority, he conceded this point also, and my Father, returning on board with his papers, sent the intruding cook to the right-about, leaving him and Mr. Piper to settle the disagreeables as well as they might.

The principle, the firmness, and the tact of my Father, in respect to the engagement and selection of his crew, were amply vindicated in the happy result of his second adventure as commander. Men who had been selected and appointed by him, readily deferred to him. Men who, contrary to ordinary slow progress, step by step, had been advanced, *per saltum*, to places of responsibility, gave spontaneous respect and honour to one who could so estimate ability, and confide in the application of untried talents. Discipline was easily preserved, and active, confiding, and cordial obedience succeeded to the former disaffection. The commanding talent of the director of the adventure thus obtained its proper scope, and resulted in an almost unprecedented measure of success.* No less than *eighteen* whales were captured, yielding 112 tuns of oil, on this, to my Father, very momentous voyage; for, whilst a second failure might have permanently blighted his hopes and prevented his prosperity, this extraordinary success directed admiring attention to the commander, who had had largeness of mind to contemplate, and superiority of ability to accomplish, so enterprising and profitable an advance beyond what his predecessors from the port of Whitby had either deemed in any way practicable, or had been limited, by their too narrow conceptions of sufficiency, from attempting.

SECTION III.—*Further Successes, with their comparative Relations, in the Ship Henrietta.*

FUTURE results clearly indicated the source, under a favouring Providence, of my Father's prosperity. These first fruits of adventure were justified by the subsequent harvest, as the legitimate proceeds of superior management. Merely accidental circumstances may yield, for an occasion or two, or for several occasions, felicitous results; but where adventures

* This measure of success, I find, had been in a trifling degree exceeded by vessels sailing from the port of Hull, but only in four instances during the preceding twenty years, comprising the enterprises of 286 ships, reckoning their repeated voyages.

involving mind and talent for their conduct, prove, through a long series of repetitions, under all the diversities of times and seasons, unusually successful, they give evidence of a master-mind directing the operations.

During the subsequent five years of my Father's enterprises in the same ship—from 1793 to 1797 inclusive,—the Henrietta's cargo stood generally, I believe, at the head of the list of successful voyages amongst the whole fleet of Greenland whalers. The least successful voyage was liberally remunerating to the owner—the most successful, unprecedentedly so. The total captures in whales, during the six successful years, including that of 1792, was no less than eighty; and the produce in oil, (considered as wonderful for that day,) 729 tuns.

Before the introduction of this species of energetic enterprise, the adventurers, as a class, were content with small things. We have the commendatory record concerning Captain Banks, of the Jenny, of Whitby, who was esteemed a talented and successful fisherman, that he brought home sixty-five whales in ten years, or six and a half per year; whereas the average captures by my Father, during the period referred to, was thirteen and one-third whales, or more than double the number of this successful predecessor.

The catch in his fifth year of command reached the then extraordinary amount of twenty-five whales; and in his last year, the proceeds in oil were greater, being 152 tuns, than had before entered the port of Whitby in any one ship.

Whilst giving the first detailed and authentic records of a Father's life and enterprises, it may be permitted, I trust, in the son, to dwell still further on these comparisons, whereby the enterprises referred to may obtain their just estimation in their bearing on the commercial prosperity of the nation.

The comparison of my Father's successes with those accustomed to be realized by the northern whale-fishers in general, will afford to him, as may have been anticipated, a highly commendatory result.

The most distinguished whale-fishers in the world, during a century and a half, or more, were the *Dutch*, with whose ordinary successes the comparison may, with propriety, first be made. Within the long interval of 107 years, ending with 1778, the produce of 57,590 whales was brought into Holland by 14,167 ships, (reckoning repeated voyages,) yielding an average of four and one-fifteenth whales per ship. During the ten years more immediately preceding my Father's commencement,—from 1769 to 1778, for instance,—the average produce of the Dutch *Greenland* whale-fishery, per ship, a year, (ninety ships, on an average being employed,) was about three and a half "fish." In the ten years beginning with 1779, (sixty sail being regularly sent out,) the average was about three and three-quarters. And in the ten years, from 1785 to 1794, passing within the period of my Father's early enterprises, (sixty ships being then also annually engaged in the fisheries of Greenland and Davis' Strait), the catch was 2294 whales, giving an average of three and eight-tenths whales per ship for each year. Hence my Father's success, compared with these various averages of the Dutch fleet, rises, in respect of the number of whales captured, in the remarkable proportion of above three and a half to one.

But we turn to *home* comparisons, which as to the object in view is of more importance to us,—though the materials for obtaining *general* results are, I regret to find, but very scanty.

As to the whale-fishery of *Great Britain*, in 1787 and 1788, we find (*Arctic Regions*, ii. p. 112,) 505 cargoes were obtained in the two years, amounting to 15,894 tuns of oil, or 31·5 tuns per ship a year.

The records in hand of the Greenland fishery from *Scotland*, in the years just preceding my Father's commencement, relate only to the period from 1785 to 1788. In each of the two latter years, when thirty-one ships were employed in the trade, the average success per ship was only two and four-fifths whales. The general average for Scotland seems, indeed, at this period to have been low; but, soon after the commencement of the present century, the enterprise and perseverance of our northern sailors began, not only to assert their proper position, but to recompense for past inferiority,—their whale-fishery of these more recent times becoming second to none, either in the ability with which it was pursued, or the success with which it was rewarded.

With the port of Whitby, from whence the Henrietta sailed, we have already drawn certain comparisons. We only add the general result of the fishery of 1786, 1787, and 1788, when twenty ships sailed from this port yearly for Greenland. The catch per ship, for each of these years, was about three and a half whales ; but, including the next three years, one of which was most disastrous, the average catch would hardly reach three fish per ship.

But the best comparisons of my Father's successes are with those of the Greenland whalers from *Hull ;* these comparisons being rendered most satisfactory because of the ample records before me of the whale fishery of that port. The records referred to are comprised in an elaborate and carefully kept manuscript, kindly entrusted to me for the present object, belonging to Mr. James Simpson, painter, of Hull, in which an admirable abstract is preserved of the whale-fishing enterprise of the port during a consecutive period of fifty-nine years, from 1772 to 1830 inclusive.

From this document, for the comparison at present designed, we obtain the following information :—
During the twenty years, from 1772 to 1791, reaching my Father's commencement, 266 ships (including repeated voyages) sailed from Hull to the Greenland whale-fishery, and obtained, altogether, an amount of produce of 9377 tuns of oil, averaging 35·25 tuns a voyage for each ship.   In the six years *before* my Father's commencement, — 1786 to 1791,—158 ships

(gross amount) obtained 4975 tuns of oil, or 31·5 on the average. And in the next six years, corresponding exactly with those of my Father's successful enterprise in the Henrietta,—1792 to 1797,—ninety-two Greenland whalers, from Hull, procured 5464 tuns of oil, or 59·4 tuns per ship a year.

My Father's average success, taken in comparison of these various *home* results, we hence gather, was about *four times* as great as the ordinary success (within the limited periods specified) of the British whalers generally. It was also *four times* as great as the usual average of the *Whitby* whalers; in like proportion above the average of the *Hull* whalers during the previous twenty years; and more than double the Hull average for the same actual period!

But to institute the most *severe* comparison with the successes of his competitors in this important field of commercial enterprise, we may notice that during the period of his command of the Henrietta (omitting, for reasons already assigned, the first year only), the amount of my Father's cargoes exceeded, by 151 tuns of oil, that of the most successful of the Hull ships of the time, amongst more than fifteen annual competitors; and was larger even than the amount attained by the six united cargoes of the most successful ship out of the whole of the whalers from the port, taken year by year! And, it is believed, could the comparison have been made with the entire fleet of whalers proceeding from Britain to the Greenland fishery, my Father, under this severest possible test of competition, with all the disadvantages of time and chance against him, would still be found at the head!

Among the captains of the Whitby fleet, no one, I believe, at all approached his successes; and among those commanding the Greenland whalers of Hull none came at all near him, except one—Captain Allan,—whose name I feel it but justice to record as the most successful fisherman of his port, and one of the first of his day. Captain Angus Sadler, whose remarkable successes we hereafter notice, did not commence until 1796. And Captain John Marshall, who afterwards became so celebrated among his compeers, was but, as yet, rising towards superiority; besides, his enterprises, after he became so signally successful, were conducted in Davis' Strait,—a branch of the fishery to which our comparison may not fairly extend.

The result of the enterprise of the other captains of this period was, in each case, so far below that of the subject of these memorials, as only, in two or three cases, to reach one-half his success. Captain Taylor, of the Fanny, brought home 400 tuns of oil within those six years, and Captain Wilson, of the Caroline, 318; but my Father's catch, as above stated, yielded no less an amount than 729 tuns! And when it is understood that the Henrietta was of but small tonnage, (254 tons,) whilst many of the Hull ships were from 50 to 100, or even 120, tons larger, the comparison instituted becomes the more remarkable.

In these successes of my Father, the people of
Whitby felt an universal and exciting interest, for
most of the principal inhabitants, as well as a large
body of those in the middle and lower classes, were,
more or less, directly or indirectly, participators in
the gains of the whale-fishery. But whilst all were
astonished at the results of enterprises so unquestionably due to an individual guidance, no small
number were moved to feelings of jealousy in consequence of successes, to which the fruits of their
personal ventures in other ships bore no reasonable
proportion. The modes in which this baneful feeling towards my Father was evinced, were as various
as they were sometimes annoying. At first, the
extraordinary results were ascribed to " luck ;" and,
subsequently, when more than luck was too obvious
to be denied, the waning phantom of superstition
was resorted to in order to escape the commendation
of a frank acknowledgment of superior merit. Some
persons there were of an order of mind so simple, as
actually to believe what was jocosely told, that he
" knee-banded" a portion of fish in one year to facilitate the success of the next. Jeers and lampoons
were made use of as outlets for the expression of
narrow and jealous selfishness,—annoyances which the
substantiality of my Father's advantages enabled him
very well to bear, but which were often keenly felt
when played off against the less stern materials of
his amiable and tender-minded wife and susceptible
young family.

The working of this principle, in envious manifestations of word and feeling, presents a painfully characteristic fruit of human degeneration from original perfectness. And the manner and sphere of its working yield very characteristic instruction on the nature of the deteriorated mind. Mankind can well bear, and be free to commend in generous frankness, successful enterprise in *other* departments than that of their own sphere. Nay, by a strange concession of the secret mind, when under a disposition to withhold the meed of praise in the department which trenches on self-interest, or self-consequence, we find many disposed to bestow an utterly extravagant measure of adulation, where it may be popular to do so, on individuals and enterprises distinctly separate and remote from interferences with themselves. But let a man be "ploughing in the same field" of enterprise, or intelligent research; let the admired results of the labour of one but stand out on the sculptured tablet of fame in bold relief of the mere groundwork surface of the other explorers of like mysteries ; or let the profitable fruits of the industry of one contrast with the sad failures or meagre successes of others engaged in the self-same species of enterprise, and then we shall find, more or less developed, among the many whose efforts have been overtopped and eclipsed, and among the multitudes, perhaps, associated relatively or interestedly with the mortified competitors, the feelings of envy and jealousy, sometimes of hatred and malice, most sadly conspicuous and dominant.

In my Father's case, where sometimes the owners, captains, and crews of near a dozen ships sailing from the same port had their most ardent enterprises, year by year, altogether eclipsed by his superior success,—and where, by reason of relative or interested association, the majority of a town's population became participators in the mortifying competition,— the measure in which the ungenerous feelings might possibly have their existence and impulses, may be well imagined to have been very extensive. That it was so in an extraordinary degree in the early progress of my Father's adventures, and during many years of his singular prosperity, every member of his family had too painful evidence.

But as to the observant and intelligent classes separate from this baneful prejudice, and as to some of more dignified minds amongst parties who were personally interested in whale-fishing concerns, the character and merits of the subject of these records were sufficiently appreciated and acknowledged.

The fame of his successes reached throughout the commercial ports of the realm, and applications of a very tempting nature came unsolicited upon him, for transferring his guidance and energies to other associates in Arctic enterprise, with encouraging promise of far more profitable results.

My Mother, who was much attached to Whitby, as a place of residence, viewed these repeated offers with much anxiety, feeling that my Father's taking a command elsewhere must involve her either in the trial of leaving Whitby, or in the great inconvenience of a much more considerable period of severance than the mere Greenland voyage required, of the family circle. For awhile her objections prevailed; but ultimately, as in another chapter we shall have to record, these objections sunk under the advantages elsewhere proffered.

SECTION IV.—*Episodical Incident—the Rescue of endangered Pleasurers.*

BEFORE carrying forward the records of my Father's new adventures in a more promising field for his personal prosperity, I shall introduce an incident of a very peculiar and interesting description, belonging to the period, though not to the business of the fishery, whilst he still held his command of the "good ship" Henrietta. It occurred whilst the ship lay at anchor, incidentally, in the river Tees, on one of her most successful voyages, homeward bound, when I was myself on board. Though I was but a child, I remember the time well. The novelty of my position in being taken on shipboard by my Father, when, a few days before, he had been on shore at Whitby, and the interesting circumstance, to me, of the capture of a small sand-bird, which I anxiously fed and endeavoured to keep alive, made an indelible impression on my youthful recollection. The incident, however, constituting the present story, I did not well understand till long afterward, but which I now record with

much confidence of being substantially correct in
every detail, from hearing it repeatedly related in
after-life.

The incident consisted in the interesting and gratifying circumstance of the saving of the lives of two
individuals moving in an upper sphere in society, by
my Father's habitual facility and accuracy in the use
of the pocket telescope, and by the information derived
therefrom being made use of with his characteristic
forethought and energetic promptness of action.

The success of the voyage had been such that the
largest amount of whales yet captured in the then
progress of the fishery, being twenty-five in number,
had enriched by their produce this single adventure.
Beyond the capacity of the *casks* taken out for the
reception of the cargo, a large quantity of blubber "in
bulk," or in massive flitches, had been stowed on the
top. The draught of water of the ship, thus unusually
loaded, was found on their arrival in Whitby Roads,
which was just after the spring-tides had passed off,
to be too great for the flow in the harbour. Whilst
waiting the advance of the succeeding spring-tides,
therefore, the ship was taken northward to the river
Tees, the nearest accessible port, and a supply of
empty casks sent thither by a small coaster, whereby
the men were usefully and savingly occupied throughout the interval in chopping up the loose blubber,
from which its valuable contents in oil were perpetually oozing out, and securing it from further waste
in the auxiliary casks.

Whilst this operation was still in active and *greasy* progress, my Father, in walking the deck, remarked on a large patch of sand, about a mile from the ship, a gig, occupied by a gentleman and a lady, driving pleasantly up and down. The day was fine, and the recreation of driving on a smooth and extended surface of sand, so singularly firm that the wheels did not penetrate beyond the slightest impression, was very enjoyable. But, as it soon appeared, and as my Father providentially anticipated, it was by no means—on the place selected—a *safe* recreation.

The bank of sand referred to, of which there are many such within the wide extent of the Tees, appeared uncovered at about half ebb, and became accessible soon afterward by the drying of a slightly depressed channel lying betwixt it and the shore. Previous to this time of tide the party had been driving nearer the fields; but tempted by the fine smooth expanse of surface of the outer sand, and encouraged by its admirable firmness on trial, they forthwith limited their driving to the breadth of the continuous surface, and continued to enjoy themselves in this recreation and their social converse, unconscious of danger, till after the tide had long been rising.

My Father, who continued observing them anxiously with his glass, had noticed the rapid rising of the tide, which he soon found was entering the channel, and separating them unconsciously from the shore. Engrossed as they seemed in their pleasant recreation, he inferred, and that justly, that their lives would soon be imperilled. Anticipating the danger, he ordered a boat to be got ready to push off at a moment's notice, should the absorbing inattention of the strangers continue. At length he saw that they had become aware of their position, and were driving their vehicle into the narrow channel into which the tide had recently flowed. With palpitating anxiety he perceived that the water was deeper than they had imagined, and that the previously firm ground, disintegrated by the action of the tide, had turned into the treacherous quicksand. He then saw the horse take alarm, the gig sink down to the axles of its wheels, and the lady and gentleman jump out in obvious terror behind, and with difficulty regain the broad surface of the yet dry, and, happily for them, firm sandbank.

Promptly he summoned the crew of the boat, whom he had previously advised of the probable result of this adventure, and sent them off with the urgent and stimulating command, "Pull as for your lives, or they will be lost!" Bravely and humanely did the sailors perform their cheerfully undertaken task: every nerve was strained to give speed to the boat, whilst the steersman, as he is wont in the pursuit of the whale, no doubt urged their nervous and energetic efforts by the oft-reiterated cry "Give way! Give way, or they will be lost!"

With intense anxiety and interest my Father watched every oar's stroke in the progress of the boat, and every action of those whose rescue he sought. He marked the gradual rise of the tide, till it just washed the highest part of the surface on which the dismayed party now stood. He perceived that the sand became softened, and that they began to sink; but, with a well-tutored judgment, he marked also, to his heart's great joy, that the boat would be in time. It approached them as they were gradually sinking, when the lady threw herself forward in the water to anticipate the rescue, and both in a few moments exulted, with nervous trepidation, in their now conscious safety from a justly-dreaded watery grave. It was a touching, heart-stirring result, realized as well by the author, under Providence, of the timely relief, as by the generously sympathising sailors and the parties themselves.

They were of course conveyed at once to the safety of the proximate shore, and, being landed there, the seamen returned to look after their horse and gig, which were all but submerged. The horse, with no small difficulty, they got disengaged from its entanglement with the vehicle, which, fortunately, had still energy enough left to enable them to swim it to the shore. The gig was then sought after, secured, and floated to the same place of safety. And, ultimately, the horse was reharnessed by their active aid; and the two individuals, who had experienced such a providential rescue, drove forthwith away from the scene of this memorable adventure.

The gentleman was found to be a Mr. M——, nephew to a dignitary of the Cathedral Church at

York; his companion, Mrs. S——, a lady of fortune. The wife of the one, I understood, and the husband of the other, were also spending the morning together mutually reciprocating in a social drive; but they had chosen the common road of the highway, and, of course, ran no risk of a similar adventure.

One would have been glad to have had to record, in connection with such an unusual incident, that the preservation from a premature death, by the sailors' cheerfully devoted energies, had met with something like a grateful recognition of the service rendered. The only acknowledgment, however, which was made for this timely and momentous aid, whereby a carriage and horse, besides the lives of two individuals in a genteel position in society were saved, was the reward of a guinea to be divided amongst the whole boat's crew. The high-minded philanthropist feels sufficient reward in the satisfaction of being privileged to be the instrument of yielding distinguished benefits to his fellow-creatures; but every right-minded person loves to see some fitting evidence of a grateful apprehension of benefits conferred. As to the paltry offering to the sailors, I remember my Father being grieved and vexed,—vexed that they should have condescended to accept any reward, where the offering, in reference even to the efforts made, much less to the service conferred, was so contemptible. As for my Father himself, the opportunity of saving the lives of two of his fellow-creatures was the source, in itself, of fervent and permanent satisfaction, affording him, no doubt, one of the most peculiarly pleasant and grateful recollections of his adventurous life.

SECTION VI.—*The Greenland Doctor.*

SOME circumstances of a more playful nature belonging to the period embraced by the present chapter may here be introduced, with a view to vary and perhaps enliven these parental records.

The subject I select belongs to the history of a kind of *steward-surgeon,*—the humble class of medical practitioners usually employed at the period of my Father's early career, being designed, on the one part, to fulfil the technical requirements of the law, that a whale-ship claiming the advantage of the Government "bounty," must carry a surgeon; and, on the other part, to gratify the officers in the captain's cabin by the improvement of the common culinary operations of the ship's cook, by the hands of the doctor or second-mate acting as cabin-steward and pastry-cook. To my Father's credit, however, it should be stated, that he was the first, as I have understood, who sought out a more fitting person for this department, and, obtaining a medical student from Edinburgh, employed him strictly as a medical officer, and gave him the advantage of a gentleman's position.

On one occasion, during the period referred to, my Father had not succeeded, when the time for the arrangement became pressing, in engaging a surgeon for the voyage. Hearing, however, of a person living in a village near Whitby, who had, according to repute, sundry qualifications appropriable to the station as its *duties* were then ordered, my Father sent to inquire whether he would like a situation, the emoluments of which might far exceed his usual earnings from a multifarious profession. The " doctor," (as we shall hereafter call him,) forthwith proceeded to Whitby, and, on being particularly questioned as to his various capabilities, gave a most ample schedule of the duties he was qualified to undertake. He could bleed and draw teeth—the two essentials for the surgeon;—he could shave and dress hair—the qualifications of the barber;—he could make pastry and bake—the chief requisites of the cabin cook.

But, in order to his passing the mustering-officer of the Customs, a medical certificate, to be obtained only by personal examination, he, somewhat to his discomfiture, was told would be requisite. After some consideration, as to the difficulties of such an ordeal, and the probabilities of failure or success, he expressed his willingness to submit to an examination. Whatever his anxieties might have been, in prospect of the trial, my father could hardly be less solicitous than the doctor himself about the result, as the sailing of the ship might possibly be delayed if the present candidate for the post of medical-officer should fail.

An appointment was forthwith arranged for this

serious affair, Doctor R——, of Whitby, being the
examiner, and the Angel Inn, the place for the
exercise. My Father, who had accompanied his
candidate officer to the place of meeting, sent him,
under guidance of a waiter, to a private room, where
Dr. R—— was waiting for him, wishing him, with
no small measure of anxious misgivings, good-luck
in his examination. But the doctor was a *wise* man,
and his simple-minded forethought did him essential
service.

In a very few minutes, to my Father's much surprise and disappointment, as he naturally anticipated,
the doctor returned "How is this?" he exclaimed,
"What is the matter, that you have returned so
soon?" "Oh," said the doctor, with a curious mix-
ture of expression of subdued happiness and self-
sufficient gratulation, "it's all over—I've passed."
"Passed!" ejaculated my Father, "how is that possible? Doctor R—— had no time to examine you."
The doubt was settled by the handing over of a slip
of paper containing a sufficient certificate. All curi-
osity to know how such an issue could have been
attained in so limited a space of time, my Father
impatiently asked, "But how was it, doctor? How
were you examined?"

The doctor described the scene, as I well remember
my Father's account of it, in about the following
terms :—"When I went to Doctor R.," said the now
happily appointed surgeon, "I spoke first; I said to
him, Doctor R , the long and the short of the busi-

E

ness is this—*if I can do no good, I'll do no harm.*"
" Then," after a moment's pause and consideration,
with some little expression of cool surprise, as the
candidate described it, " Then," replied the examiner, " *you'll do better than half the doctors in
England;*" and, without a word more, he proceeded
to write out a certificate.

Anecdotes of the doctor were not unfrequently
told, with evident pleasant recollections, by my Father,
who seemed, in an unusual degree, to have exercised
a playful pleasantry with this simple-minded officer of
many departments.

The cookery he managed with a fair measure of
ability; and the breakfast cakes, though not always
so *fair* as they might have been, were sufficiently
enjoyable in comparison of hard coarse biscuits.
But a little disrelish was threatened by an accidental sight of the process of cake-making, which
it required the full measure of indifference to trifling
unfitnesses among the sailors of the mess to get over.
One morning, early, my Father happened to pass by
the place where the doctor was industriously preparing the paste for the oven. To his surprise he
observed, and uttered an exclamation expressive of
the surprise, that the hands of the manipulator of the
elements of bread were not only unwashed, but most
remote from the ordinary colour belonging to clean-
liness. The doctor bore the exclamation with the
coolest perseverance, and without even lifting his

eyes from the bowl in which he was mixing the
materials, contented himself with remarking, in re-
duplication of expression, the but ill-consoling fact,
as to the effect of the operation on his hands, " the
paste will clean them ! the paste will clean them !"

The doctor was ambitious of practice in shooting,
and fond of embracing occasions for the purpose.
Whilst the ship was incidentally lying close beset
in the ice, without the possibility of any movement
being effected, my Father, on one occasion, be-
thought himself of an enlivenment of the general
depression incident to such a situation, at the expense of the simple-hearted, good-natured doctor.
For this he made the fitting arrangements, and then,
calling up the doctor, pointed him out a dark-looking
object, apparently a seal, lying at some little distance
from the ship, and asked him if he would like to go
and try to shoot it ? The proposition was too pleasant to the doctor's wishes to be rejected, and preparations were forthwith made by the bringing up
of two guns, with the requisites for loading, upon
the deck. My Father took one of the guns to load,
handing over the other to the doctor for the same
purpose, and then they descended upon the ice, which
afforded a sufficiently firm footing for their travelling
to the place where the object of the contemplated
sport was seen.

As they proceeded, my Father favoured the doctor
by offering him the first shot; but supposing his own

gun might suit the doctor best, being a finer and lighter piece than the other, he proposed an exchange, which was readily and thankfully accepted.

Coming near the place, they saw the dark-looking back of the creature plainly appearing, with an occasional slight movement indicative of wakefulness, behind a small hummock of the ice; then advancing cautiously, till almost within shot, my Father suggested that the doctor should creep forward, in shelter of the hummock, till he got the animal sufficiently within command of his gun. Having attained the requisite position, my Father, in an audible whisper, cried, "Now, doctor, now's your time!" The doctor having anxiously taken his aim, and satisfactorily covered the creature with his gun, fired, when, instead of a seal, up started one of the seamen, uttering a terrific shout of "Murder! murder! I'm a murdered man!" My Father joined in the exclamation of horror at what the doctor had done; and the doctor turning ashy pale, his knees tottering and his teeth chattering from terror, had well nigh fallen insensible under his acute emotions—emotions aggravated in intenseness of anxiety, by the cries of the other seamen now rushing in a body to the place, to see the sad catastrophe of "a man shot in mistake for a seal by the fool of a doctor."

Happily for the dismayed and suffering sportsman, the catastrophe, though almost too painful as a joke, was soon proved to be exaggerated and unreal, by the supposed wounded seaman throwing aside the deceptive character he had assumed, and coming forward to join in the laugh against him.

It is hardly necessary to mention that the whole affair was contrived, and that, by the changing of guns, my Father had secured the well-charged one of the doctor's, and replaced it with one abundantly furnished with powder and wadding, but devoid altogether of deadly shot.

It is seldom that practical jokes go off so well; for few persons will be content to be made the dupe for others' entertainment. The potion, therefore, that we should not like to have given sportively unto ourselves, we should be cautious in administering to others. Manifold cases of very serious mischief, extending even to results fatal to human life, have arisen from the unfitting or unseasonable playing off of practical jokes. In the case which I have ventured to describe, however, there was little risk. The position of the author of the joke in respect to that of its subject, on the one part, and the good-natured simplicity of character of the subject on the other, afforded, together, a sufficient security against any essential mischief. Perhaps, too, where an entire ship's company were in much depression of mind, by reason of the alarming and tedious besetment under which they were suffering, a beneficial and redeeming effect was, on the whole, realised. For the doctor himself, so far from cherishing any painful or unkindly feelings on account of the part he had unconsciously played in the little facetious drama, was too happy in being relieved from the temporarily imagined misery of having, whilst seeking sport, deprived a fellow-creature of life. So effective, indeed, did this influence react upon his feelings of anxiety, that he himself joined in the general hilarity as heartily as any of his amused shipmates.

SECTION VI.—*Taming of a Bear—Interesting Recognition.*

THE *Polar Bear* is popularly known as one of the strongest and most ferocious of that class of animals which shrinks not from voluntary conflict with man. The species is often met with, sometimes in considerable numbers, upon the shores of the Arctic lands, and within the region of the ices of the Greenland sea. It not unfrequently occurs of the length of seven or eight feet, and four or five feet high, weighing as much as a small ox. Specimens whose skin measured twelve to thirteen feet in length, have been described by voyagers. The "paw of the bear," of which there is Scriptural mention, may, in the full-grown animal, as now met with, be from seven to nine inches in breadth, and large enough to overspread two-thirds of a square foot, or more, of the snowy surface on which it treads. Hence its admirable adaptation for the region in which Providence has placed its abode.

Of this animal the Arctic whaler has frequent opportunities of making captures, and, sometimes, of adding a stirring variety to the ordinary scenes of conflict and adventure. My Father's experience, whilst affording many examples of the former result, had a reasonable share of the latter. It is to a special case, however, as indicated in our head-title, that the present record relates.

On one occasion, when a female bear with cubs had been attacked, one of the young ones was taken alive. It was a fine, and, for a cub, well-grown animal. When first taken on board, it was temporarily secured on an unoccupied part of the deck, but in a place near to which my Father had incidentally to pass. Whilst thus passing, inconsiderate about any risk of assault, the animal very unexpectedly made a spring at him, but fortunately, checked by his rope, failed in the ferocious intent. This circumstance suggested the idea, which he soon proceeded to carry out, not only of chastising, but of subduing the captive animal. The proceeding adopted was as follows :—

The rope already encircling the neck of the bear was put through a ring-bolt on the deck, and the head was thereby drawn so closely down as to limit its capabilities of extension within the range of a few inches, or perhaps about a foot. My Father then took his station in a secure position, and held out his hand invitingly towards it, an action which the irritated creature retorted by a furious roar, and attempt to bite. This act he rebuked by striking it over the snout with the fingers, closely compacted, of one of his hands. At each blow, attempts were vainly made to catch and tear the audacious instrument by which Bruin was thus being chastised. But after very many repetitions of the now keenly-felt strokes of the hand on this tender place of the head, and after as many failures, on the part of the chastised creature, in his endeavours to retaliate, the bear began evidently to feel a commanding influence, as indicated by the frequent effort to avoid the coming blow. Occasionally, however, he would renew his attempts to bite, roaring, with an obviously mixed expression of ferocity and pain. Perseveringly, as the bear continued to resist, the same chastisement was regularly administered, till at last, the recently intractable animal began to be subdued under the master-power with which he struggled.

The effect of the process was, from time to time, tested, by holding out a finger near to the creature's face. If it attempted to bite, the chastisement was continued until, on the application of the test, there was either a quiet submission, or a turning away of the head. Ultimately the animal was made acquainted with our accustomed modes of expressing approbation, by being patted on the neck or side of the head; and, then, as often as it rebelled, the usual punishment was renewed, and, whenever it indicated submission, it either received the former token of approval, or the more substantial and intelligible reward of being fed by the hand by which it had been wont to be chastised.

The thorough subjection, indeed, of this naturally ferocious creature was soon effected,—within the

space, I believe, of two or three days,—and from
that time forward my Father's command over it was
uniform and supreme. Nor was the kindness with
which he treated the captive lost upon it; for it yielded,
as occasions permitted, very decided indications of
an inversion of its ordinary vicious propensities in
respect to its considerate master. Two illustrative cases
belong to this record.

On the arrival of the ship in port, bruin was removed to the oil-yard,—the premises on which the
blubber was landed, in order to its being reduced into
marketable oil. Its arrival became a subject of
popular interest, and the inhabitants of Whitby
flocked out in masses to see it.

Whilst so situated, the bear, somehow or other,
obtained his release, and escaped into an adjoining
covert,—" Cockmill Wood." The incident soon became known at Whitby. A wild and dangerous
animal—now rendered supremely ferocious by reason
of the almost perpetual teazing to which he had been
subjected from his numerous visitors—at large, within
a mile or so of the town, and in a wood intersected by
a much-frequented footpath, proved the occasion of
great and general excitement. Men and lads, assisted
by dogs, and armed with guns and a variety of other
destructive weapons, were speedily in progress, and
with overwhelming superiority, towards the retreat of
the bear, with a view to its destruction.

Happily for poor Bruin, my Father got timely intimation of the circumstance that had occasioned so

much alarm. He proceeded forthwith to the oil-yard, where he provided himself with a short piece of rope, and then climbed the cliff into the wood in search of the stray animal. Guidance was sufficiently afforded by the stream of persons flowing towards the place of his retreat, and, on nearer approach, by the noise and clamours of the assemblage.

It was a curious scene. A motley crowd of men and boys and dogs formed, at a respectable distance, a curvilinear front, with the surprised object of attack quietly standing in the focus. Fortunately no blood had yet been shed; no wounds or bruises yet given. It was the important moment of mutual reconnoissance. It might have been a question how the creature should be dealt with? Whether he should be summarily attacked with fire-arms, or, by the help of the restrained dogs, his recapture attempted?

Any doubts which might have thus occasioned the desirable delay were now speedily settled. My Father, with only the rope in his hand, made his appearance. He passed through the ranks of the would-be warriors in the contemplated fight; when, to their utter amazement, and to the no small alarm of many, he proceeded without hesitation forward. Speaking to the bear, in his usual manner, as he approached, and walking straight up to him, face to face, he patted the shaggy neck, as he placed a prepared noose of the rope around it, and then quietly led away the furious brute, which, under his commanding guidance, became as tractable as a lap-dog!

The other incident connected with this animal is worthy of record, being, if somewhat less adventurous, not less curious.

The care-taking and maintenance of a now considerably grown Polar bear soon became matter of inconvenience. It might, there is little doubt, have been sold advantageously for being itinerated as a *show* about the country; but my Father imagined a destination for it, where it would be better cared for, by having it deposited along with the wild beasts in the Tower.

It being ascertained that the contribution would be very acceptable, the bear was embarked in a coaster. On its arrival in the Thames, it was received in a manner befitting its importance and security, and safely transferred to its final destination.

It was about a twelvemonth or more, I believe, after Bruin's regular installation among the wild beasts of the National collection, that my Father, happening to be in London, determined on taking a look at his old acquaintance, Bruin. Proceeding to the Tower, he paid the usual entrance-fee, and without intimating anything about his special object, took the course through the collection, like other visitors, as guided by the exhibitor.

His eye being wistfully directed in advance of his position, he at length got sight of the looked-for object; when, breaking away from those pursuing the prescribed progress, he hurried directly up to where his ursine friend was encaged. A warning cry came

urgently from the keeper, who had noticed his near
and bold approach to a place of danger—" Take care,
sir, that is one of the most ferocious animals in the
collection;" but it was disregarded.   My Father only
paused, whilst, by his familiar and accustomed salu-
tation,—" Poor Bruin! poor fellow!"—he gained the
attention of the animal, when, catching its eye, and
perceiving he was recognised, he went quietly up,
thrust his arm through the cage, and, whilst he patted
the neck and head of the evidently delighted creature,
received a species of fawning response, which was
eloquently interesting and touching.   The keeper, who
had rushed forward on witnessing the daring intrusion
on the interior of the bear's cage, now stood fixed
in almost speechless astonishment.   At length, lifting
his hands with a characteristic indication of his extreme amazement, he exclaimed,—" Why, sir, I never
saw the like of that all the days of my life!"

The subjection of the wildest and most ferocious
animals to the authority of man is not so much, we
may observe, the result of man's superiority as of the
Creator's special appointment.   It was His design and
command, in respect to the inferior creatures, that
this should be so.   The superiority appointed originally to Adam was, that he should " have dominion
over the fish of the sea, and over the fowl of the air,
and over every living thing that moveth upon the
face of the earth."   But the appointment, which was
simple and natural when all was innocency, was after-

wards renewed, we find, under a *new influence*, that
of *fear*, specially induced on the general constitution
of the animal creation. For among the blessings
graciously assured by the Almighty to the righteous
Noah and his sons, on their descent from the Ark,
we have this pervading influence set forth in these
characteristic terms:—" The *fear* of you, and the
dread of you shall be upon every beast of the earth,
and upon every fowl of the air ; upon all that moveth
upon the earth, and upon all the. fishes of the sea :
into your hand are they delivered."—Gen. ix. 2.

CHAPTER III.

THE SHIP "DUNDEE," OF LONDON.

SECTION I.—*Entrance on, and General Results of, this New Command.*

THE aversion of his wife to a change in the port of sailing, though it might retard, did not prevent my Father's ultimately making that change. He had been applied to by letter, and with reiterated urgency, and offers of additional advantages, by a mercantile firm in London (Messrs. Edward Gale and Sons) to take charge of a ship of theirs, which they were anxious to employ in the northern whale-fishery. But, finding that the applications by letter failed, or at least led to no satisfactory result, one of the principals of the house determined on an application in person,—an undertaking, at that time, involving a most troublesome and tedious journey,—and, totally unexpected, made his appearance at the residence of our family in Whitby.

The circumstance of Mr. Piper's early consideration for, and confidence in, my Father, on an occasion which, under the Divine blessing, proved the turning-point of his fortune in life, had induced a feeling of regard and gratitude so decided as to become strongly resistant of the temptation to change. But, on the other

hand, he had long felt dissatisfaction at the abridgment
of some allowances and perquisites enjoyed by his
predecessor in command, and promised to himself,
which, though of but small consideration in the meagre
extent of the former wonted success, had accumulated,
in the estimation made year by year during his extraordinary successful career, to a very handsome amount,
in money value. His repeated remonstrances at this
deprivation and injustice being always met with a
" Pooh, pooh! be content; you have done very well,"
—no doubt served greatly to weaken the binding influence of ties otherwise so decidedly felt, and frankly
acknowledged. Hence, from an unwise and ungenerous policy, which, in the course of six years had
deprived my Father of a sum amounting, as he calculated, to about 300*l.* out of his rightful earnings, the
alliance previously existing betwixt himself and the
owners of the Henrietta, was, with due and honourable
notice on his part, brought to a conclusion by the visit
and liberal proposals of Mr. Gale. These proposals,
as I have understood, involved a new and additional
advantage to the commander, in a per centage upon
the value of the cargo obtained, together with the
proffer of a small share in the concern, on terms at
once equitable and easy. On this encouraging basis
an arrangement was forthwith made with the house
which Mr. Gale represented, for the command, by
my Father, of the *Dundee,* of London, a ship much
larger and finer than the Henrietta, on a whale-
fishing adventure in the Greenland seas.

In the spring of the year 1798, the Dundee, according to the arrangement made, was, after being strengthened and fortified for the navigation of the formidable ices of the north, fitted out, and set forth on her first voyage to the fishery. The result far more than realized the hopes and expectations of all the parties interested in the adventure; for, in a surprisingly short interval of time, the return of the Dundee to the Thames was announced, with the exulting and almost incredible report, that she brought the spoils of no less than *six-and-thirty* captured whales! The report proved true; and, although many of the whales were of small size, yet a quantity of produce, in oil and whalebone, such as no other adventurer had hitherto obtained, was yielded by this extraordinary "catch."

During subsequent adventures, with but one exception in a series of five years, my Father's high reputation for pre-eminent skill and success, was amply maintained. In one of these voyages (that of 1801) twenty-three whales were captured, which yielded the previously unequalled quantity of 225 tuns of oil;* and the voyage following, which terminated his command of the Dundee, produced twenty whales, yielding 200 tuns of the best kind of train oil, with a proportional weight of whalebone.

These voyages were not only unequalled in the

---

* Up to the end of the eighteenth century my Father's successes, with but rare exceptions, were at the head of the list of the whole of the northern whalers, both of Davis' Strait and Greenland. But about this period Captain Marshall, in the Davis'-Strait branch, began to take the lead of all competitors there.

Greenland whale-fishery in their measure of success, but likewise in the quickness with which they were accomplished. *Ordinarily*, my Father's ship, not sailing earlier than his competitors in general, not only brought home the largest cargo of any in the fleet, but returned amongst the soonest. The produce in oil, therefore, partly from the freshness of the blubber when it was brought to the "coppers," and partly from the care taken, under his direction, in the process of boiling, was, as I have advisedly designated it, of the *best quality*.

SECTION II.—*Dangerous Accident—Admirable Tact.*

WHILST pursuing for a long series of years, so adventurous a profession as that of the whale-fishery, accidents of a peculiar nature were not unfrequently occurring. On such occasions, my Father's promptness and judiciousness of action were as admirable as they were characteristic.

But leaving such incidents, as far as may be, to their place, chronologically, in our present Memorials, we adduce here a single example, which may serve at once to illustrate and to justify this observation. The case, indeed, though pertaining to his professional pursuits, did not occur when at sea; but during the process of reducing the blubber of the whale into oil, after the return of the ship into port.

The ship Dundee, whilst commanded by my Father,

had but recently returned from one of her usually
successful voyages, and was laid, for discharging at
the quay, in Blackwall Dock, near to the premises in
which the oil was being boiled. My Father, during the
most active part of the operations of discharging and
boiling, was in the habit of sleeping on board the ship;
and, at the time of the accident referred to, I, then a
boy, happened to be with him. Sometime during the
night, we were all awoke by loud and fearful shrieking,
from the direction of the boiling-house. My Father,
instantly apprehending some accident there, jumped
from his bed, and, just as he was, flew up on deck
and over the ship's side, and in a few moments of
time was at the spot from whence the shrieks proceeded. The idea that had at once flashed upon his
mind was appallingly realized. One of the poor
fellows, engaged at the reducing of the blubber, was
in the condition of being dragged out of the boiling
cauldron by his associate in the work!

My Father's most powerful helping hand was
opportunely available, and, with the quickness of
thought, he plunged the appalled sufferer into a large
cistern of cold oil and blubber, resting on the platform above the copper,—a cistern, or "beck," as it
is called, out of which the contents of the copper,
after being boiled and emptied, were to be renewed.
In this most appropriate bath, the poor fellow was for
a considerable time kept immersed. My impression
is that he was kept there until means were obtained
for his removal; and then he was conveyed, without

further delay, to the London Hospital. His life, notwithstanding the terrible severity, was thus happily saved. My Father's conduct was highly commended and applauded by the medical staff of the Hospital, both for his discernment of the best treatment, perhaps, which could have been administered, and for his so promptly giving the sufferer the advantage of it.

The cause of this appalling accident, was, I believe, the breaking of the staff of the stirrer, which the night-watch over the boiling was required to have continually in motion, to prevent the "finks" (the cellular substance of the blubber) sticking to the bottom or sides of the copper when boiling. By the sudden failure of the staff, against which he pressed his shoulder, he was projected forward, but, providentially, not so as to fall headlong,—his effort to recover himself so far succeeding as to cause him to plunge feet foremost, whilst he sunk, on attempting to reach the shelving side of the copper, up to the waist in the horrible bath!

I yet remember, young as I then was, the return of the debilitated but happy sufferer, after his discharge, "as cured," from the Hospital. The man, whom I had known familiarly as a stout, lively, good-natured fellow, was now reduced into a mere shred— a poor, pallid creature, an almost skeleton of a man! But his ultimate restoration, I believe, was quite complete. He knew and appreciated the wisdom with which he had been treated—he felt and acknowledged that to my Father, under Providence, he owed his life.

Section III.—*The Dandy Sailor; or, " Fine Tommy."*

In this connection, whilst now story-telling, we may perhaps, as fittingly as elsewhere, introduce a little record, very often told by my Father, for enforcing a moral lesson in respect of a species of folly which we often witness, and from which some of my young readers, peradventure, may not find themselves entirely devoid.

If the sacrifice of personal comfort to the tyranny of fashion appeared to my Father a great absurdity; much more did the risking of health for the indulgence of personal conceit in dress, or the braving of severity of climate, inadequately clothed, from the vanity of singularity in hardiness, seem to him as the very summit and extravagance of folly.

It was in support of his views on this particular subject, when conspicuous instances of such folly happened to come before him, that my Father was wont to tell, as an impressive warning, the instructive story of " Fine Tommy."

Fine Tommy, who had acquired this appellation by particularity and almost dandyism of dress when at sea, was a smart and well-looking youthful sailor, who had shipped himself with my Father in one of the voyages in which he commanded the " Dundee." His personal conceit, so unusual with the thoroughbred sailor, was nevertheless associated in him with such a measure of activity and seamanlike acquire-

ments, as to save him from that ridicule of his associates, which in any other case would have been
excessive, if not intolerable. Whilst the temperature
of the weather was but moderately severe, his appearance on deck in a smart light shore-going jacket,
exposed him to little damage beyond the playful
salutations of his comrades, — salutations which he
was wont good-humouredly to return by speaking
with indifference of the hitherto experienced cold,
and ridiculing the feminine weakness of a premature
muffling of the person with pea-jackets, huge boots,
comforters, and mittens.

During most of the progress of the ship northward,
Fine Tommy continued successfully and proudly to
brave, as I have just intimated, the gradually increasing cold, and that without material inconvenience
or damage. But at length, when the region of ice
had been some little way penetrated, the previously
prevailing southerly or temperate wind happened to
shift during the night to the northward, which, with
a fresh blowing gale, brought a rapidly lowering
temperature, approaching the zero of the thermo-
metic scale. The ship soon became covered with
ice, and a chilly penetrating "frost-rime" powdered
the hair, or (as in some cases adopted) the rough
wigs of the sailors. Before Fine Tommy's watch
was called,—for there were usually three watches in
the whale ships, affording eight hours below alternately with four upon deck,—the extreme change,
almost from a bearable frostiness to the greatest

severity of cold, had taken place. He, incredulous
of the influence as well as unconscious of the change
that had taken place, came up in his usual clothing,
a thin jacket, light shoes, and uncovered hands.
Now jeered by his watch-mates as to his perception
of cold, he determinately faced the chilling blast,
renewing his bravadoes of indifference of feeling
even to the then prevailing severity. This lasted
during his two watches for the day. All hands
besides were muffled up in every species of warm
clothing, whilst Fine Tommy still walked the deck
and performed his various duties with no other protection against the really Arctic severity of cold than
aforetime.

On the calling of the watch the following morning,
however, Fine Tommy did not appear. The next
day, too, he was absent from his station. When
his turn came to take the helm he was not there.
Enquiry was made, and my Father found, as he
had well predicted, that Fine Tommy was ill, and
obliged to keep his bed. Day after day, and week
after week, passed over, and the absent one was still
unseen. Even *months* passed over until the voyage,
which had been prospered with splendid success,
was approaching to a close, so that the attainment
of a temperate latitude and a return of warm weather
had begun to cheer our northern adventurers with
the prospect of a speedy realization of home enjoyment, when, like the hybernating insect revived by
the genial influence of the summer sun, Fine Tommy

was also resuscitated; and the long prostrate and
once foolish defier of the Arctic climate appeared
again upon deck to breathe the restorative air as it
came pure from the grand repository of the atmo-
sphere, instead of the defiled and mixed vapours of
the 'tween decks of a whale-ship.

The lesson thus impressively taught was often read
in my hearing; the application, in some cases, possibly, might be intended for myself. If one was seen
wading, as it were, in mud with a pair of light shoes
inadequate for defence either against cold or wet,—
the admonition or remark was ever prompt, "it
would be well to mind Fine Tommy." If a fashion-
able "dandy" coat, in the days of dandyism, were
worn in the severity of winter; if a dress insufficient
for protection or warmth were, by either sex, observed to be worn; if the outside of a coach were
mounted without an adequate covering, or a ride in
an open carriage undertaken with only the habili-
ments usually worn in walking, the monition became
natural, as the moral was apt,—"to remember Fine
Tommy." Whenever, too, I have myself remarked
the analogous folly, every where, indeed, more or
less observable, of risking health or abandoning personal comfort to *appearance* or *fashion*, the moral of
this very lesson has constantly been forced on my
recollection, tempting to the relation of the story,
in order to the more impressive effect of the warning,—" Remember Fine Tommy!"

SECTION IV. — *Unfortunate Voyage, and Adventure
in the Greenland Ices.*

ONE of my Father's voyages in the Dundee, and
but one in the various ships he commanded for a
period of upwards of a quarter of a century, commencing with the year 1792, proved a failure.   The
failure, however, arose from one of those incidental
circumstances of climate, on the one part, and neglect
of a principal officer, on the other part, which no
human foresight could have anticipated, or human
skill or diligence have remedied, after the perilous
character of the ice-entanglement became clearly
apparent.

This misadventure occurred, singularly enough,
when I happened, though only a boy of ten years of
age at the time, to be of the number of the souls on
board.   On the invitation of my Father, who had
landed from his ship in passing Whitby, on his progress northward, to take leave of his family, I had
gone off with him, designing to return by the pilot
boat, to see the ship.   I was astonished with what
I saw; I explored with unmixed delight every accessible compartment of the cabins and store-rooms
below, and conceived an irresistible desire to remain
where I was, and go out on the voyage.   At length
the call of the pilots for "Master William," as the
day advanced to its close, put my desire to the test of
practicability.   For a while I remained silent below,
and when silence was no longer likely to be available,

I contrived the child-like device of hiding my hat, which, on ascending the companion ladder bare-headed, I let it be understood I could not find! My Father having noticed my delight, and interpreting rightly the little device, remarked to the pilots,— "Don't mind him; he will go along with us." A mother's anguish, however, who loved me with the tenderest and most ardent affection, flashed into my mind. It forced utterance in the expression,—"But what will my Mother say?" The reply, curiously enough regarded as being consolatory, sufficed to allay my scruples,—"She will love you better when you come back!" The pilots still urging haste in my embarkation, as the boat was thumping heavily against the ship's gangway, were at length made sensible of what they at first could not credit, that I was to remain behind; and they set out for the shore in no small condition of amazement, and with no slight feeling of sympathising embarrassment, on account of the report they must yield to one, whom they sufficiently knew as an anxious, susceptible, and affectionate mother!

But my own story must be here suspended, as it possibly may hereafter find a place, if Providence yield me health and life for the undertaking, in the series of the "Memorials of the Sea," which, some-times, I venture to contemplate carrying on.

The leading incidents of this disappointing enter-prise, I am enabled to give with a satisfactory measure

of confidence, from a record made of it, many years
ago, in a private autobiography, from which, mainly,
I extract the following details.

After touching at Lerwick (Shetland), for the completion of our supplementary crew of *boatmen,* we
proceeded northward towards the usual whale-fishing
stations. On arriving in sight of Spitzbergen, and
finding the western coast accessible, with a vein of
clear water running continuously along shore, we pursued the encouraging opening as far as the northern
headland of Charles Island, in latitude 78° 53′ N.
Here, tempted by the clear water eastward, we
reached into a wide inlet near King's Bay, when, by
a sudden gale coming on from the northward and
north-westward, we were driven, encumbered by ice
of recent formation, and fragments of old ice, into
the opening betwixt the foreland and the main, where
the ship ultimately became closely beset in the *Bay
of Birds* of Barentz.

At first, the officers in general thought little of the
entanglement, expecting that any favourable change
of wind would serve to release us.   My Father,
however, watching the augmentation in the thickness
of the ice, by pressure and frost, received, very early,
a more anxious impression. He had observed, indeed,
that the ice was not yet thoroughly sealed together
and fixed into an immoveable mass. For, periodically,
he perceived, that some relaxation in the compactness
of the general body of ices took place, which he
ascribed to the action of a tide ; and, on one evening,

before retiring to rest, when a fine breeze, favourable
for promoting an opening seaward had begun to pre-
vail, he rather confidently anticipated some relaxation
which might be available for our escape at the period
of the favourably acting tide. In this expectation,
he gave special orders to the chief officer, who had
formerly been a whaling commander, and ought to
have well appreciated the importance of the instruction,—to call him when the hoped-for relaxation of
the ice might take place. But, disappointingly
enough, he awoke of himself after a rather long
sleep, when, as his watch indicated, the time of
favourable tide must be passed. He anxiously dressed
himself and hasted upon deck; but, whilst much
slack and navigable ice was yet visible at some little
distance to the north-westward, all about the ship
was close and impenetrable. His enquiry as to
whether the ice about the ship had not also slacked?
led to the mortifying admission, reluctantly extracted,
that the ice had indeed slacked very near to the ship,
but, as was intimated in excuse, " it was so *rank* and
difficult that nothing could be done without ' calling
all hands,' and much trouble; and he," the chief
mate, " thought it would perhaps be more cleared
away, by the hopeful breeze, by the time the Captain
turned out!"

The highly culpable folly of this conduct became
too soon apparent to all. For when an easterly, and
then a southerly wind blew, without inducing any
repetition of the slackness that had been missed;

when we found the whole of the accumulated ices frozen into a solid field, without crack, or opening of any kind to be seen from the mast-head; when we marked our position as deeply embayed within the projecting headlands, and the ice everywhere wedged up against and cemented to all the circumjacent shores,—every one became anxious respecting the success of the voyage, whilst some began to entertain the depressing apprehension that the ship might possibly be detained throughout the winter!

The story of our distressing detention, with the measures adopted partly for the employment of the men, but which became ultimately available, even beyond our utmost hopes, for facilitating our release, is too long,—consistently with the extent designed for this volume, and the completion hereafter, possibly, of some personal records,—for being given in detail. It may be sufficient, for our present purpose, now to say, that after the endurance of the misery of an eight weeks' besetment, release was happily attained, and the Dundee was again free (but not until the season adapted for the fishery had thus been all but wasted) to range through any part of the ordinarily accessible ocean.

Our course being directed towards the north-west, we soon fell in with ships, and learnt that the fishery had been tolerably good, and that two or three ships had already obtained almost full cargoes.

Shortly afterwards we met with fish, and all hands set forth in earnest anxious pursuit. But they were, in fact, too anxious, and, in part, discouraged by the idea that the season was about at an end. Their efforts, in consequence, were ill directed or inadequately followed up, and only mortifying failures resulted. Stimulated by the defects and failures of his harponeers, my Father was induced to try the chase himself. Forthwith taking his post at the bow of one of the boats, he soon gave evidence of his superior efficiency. He " struck " whale after whale to the amount of three; but not being adequately supported by the other boats, one of the first of these escaped from the harpoon, under circumstances such as, he considered, should have led to its capture. Excited by this failure, he changed boats, in one of the other cases, after the fish, under the first harpoon, had reappeared at the surface; and, as the harponeers generally seemed heartless and inert, he changed again, after fastening another harpoon, until he had planted no less than three or four harpoons, in the same fish, with his own hands!

The season, however, soon came to a close, and these two whales, with a dead one which was also discovered by himself, constituted the whole of the Dundee's cargo in this trying year,—a cargo yielding only five-and-forty tuns of oil, yet amounting, after all, to nearly two-thirds of the general average of the Greenland fishery.

Notwithstanding this serious abstraction from the general average of his five years' adventures in the

Dundee, my Father's general pre-eminence was, in the issue, still maintained. During these five voyages, ninety-four whales were captured, and an amount of 812 tuns of oil brought to market. The yearly average, *inclusive* of the year of unavoidable failure, was no less than 18·8 whales, producing 162·4 tuns of oil, besides the fair proportion of whalebone, seal-skins, etc.

Compared with the fishery from Hull and Whitby, and, as far as my materials go, elsewhere, this result was considerably beyond that of any other Greenland whaler. With respect to the Hull average for the same period, the Dundee's superiority was in the ratio of 162·4 to 77·5 tuns of oil, or more than two to one. In comparison with the success of any other individual ship, the Dundee still stood at the head of the list,— the nearest approach in Hull being that of the Ellison, a ship commanded, during four years out of the five, by the same enterprising and talented officer, Mr. Allan, as we had occasion to notice, so favour-ably, in a former comparison. The Molly, Captain Angus Sadler,—a hardy adventurous and able com-mander, who, in subsequent years, became chief amongst his competitors from Hull,—obtained, during my Father's command of the Dundee, the next highest amount of cargoes,—the total, in the five years, being 689 tuns of oil. The Egginton, Wray, (one voyage under another captain) obtained, at the same time, 508 tuns; the Symmetry, Rose, 481 tuns; the Fanny, Jameson and Taylor, 460 tuns; the

Manchester, Matson, 417 tuns, etc.;—the Dundee's cargoes, as has been shewn, being, in the same period, 812 tuns.

But, besides these comparisons, in all respects so favourable, we may again venture, up to the end of eleven years of consecutive adventures, to take the severest test of competition; viz. a comparison betwixt the Dundee's cargoes, and that of the select cargoes, for the five corresponding years, of the most prosperous Greenland-man, from Hull, of each year. And under this amount, being 806 tuns of oil, the Dundee is found still to stand the first.

SECTION V.—*Successful Stratagem in War.*

AN incident of a very stirring and exciting nature occurred in the very outset of the unfortunate voyage just referred to, which I here take occasion of introducing, as very characteristic of my Father's tact and cool self-possession.

A day or two after leaving the coast of Yorkshire, from whence I had myself embarked,—the weather being fine with a brisk and favourable wind, and the ship going steadily and swiftly under her ample and well-trimmed sails,—all hands were set to work, my Father superintending, in clearing the 'tween-decks of a variety of stores hastily taken in, and confusedly scattered about, in order to make all snug and secure for the North-Sea passage. So much were all hands, men and officers, engrossed by this important labour of clearance and order, that, some how or other, the "look-out" had been for awhile neglected, when, suddenly it was announced, by a voice calling out from the deck at one of the hatchways—"a ship bearing down close upon us!"

It being a time of war, and the North Sea abounding with ships of war and privateers of the enemy, the announcement produced an instant suspension of the work going on, and drew universal attention to a circumstance which might possibly involve the safety of life and property in the ship.

My Father's quick eye, and sure telescopic glance, discovered at once the characteristic marks of an enemy, and vessel of war. She was bearing down, steering easterly, exactly so as to intercept our track, but not on any of the courses usually steered either for England, France, or Denmark. Already she had approached within a little more than a mile of our position, and so that in about a quarter of an hour we must be within hailing distance.

With the promptness and coolness characteristic of the Dundee's Commander, measures for self-defence, and skilful stratagy, were arranged and progress commenced. These measures, I conceive, are worthy of some particular notice.

His habit, it should be observed, was to endeavour to anticipate, in quiet contemplation, the various contingencies pertaining to his enterprise, which, peradventure, might be considered as not unlikely to happen. The meeting of an enemy, therefore, was

one of those incidents that had been regarded as by
no means improbable, and the dealing with which,
by what ingenious tact or device might be available,
had been well considered. For to *fight* with an
enemy, where stratagy might answer for an escape,
was justly held as most unwise, where success in
conflict could gain no prize;* where failure must
issue in loss of property, voyage, and personal liberty;
and where either failure or success must probably
involve a loss of life, for which there was neither call
of duty to risk, nor possible compensation to justify.

Fortunately, had the extremity required, he was
in a position calculated for a brave defence. The
Dundee was as well armed as she was well manned,
carrying twelve guns, eighteen pounders, I believe,
with a crew of betwixt fifty and sixty men. The
guns were already loaded, and in every way fit for
immediate service.

The stratagy, in this case, contemplated, was to
give, to the threatening assailant, the surprise of a
concealed armament, and the impression as of a
designed deception in the class of ship assumed.

And fortunate it was, that there were circumstances
connected with the qualifications of the crew, and the

* Some of our readers may require to be informed, that an ordinary
merchant ship, not having "letters of marque" for acting as a privateer,
can have no claim on any property which the bravery of her captain
and crew might take from an enemy. So that, in the event of capturing an assailant, as might have been possible in the case referred
to, the hard blows and damage must be borne by the merchantman,
whilst the prize would fall due to the first ship of war incidently met
with, or otherwise to the sovereign or public officers at home.

construction of the ship, admirably adapted for the experiment proposed. For contemplating, as we have intimated, such a risk as that now threatening him, my Father had selected out of the variety of hands offering themselves for the voyage, two men of rather unusual qualifications,—one, who was an adept in beating the drum, the other "in winding a boatswain's call." These qualities, amongst seafaring men, being almost peculiar to classes employed in vessels of war, induced a preference, in respect to them, over others, though the drummer might by no means be equal to some who were rejected, in regard to general seamen-like attainments.

The construction of the ship, too, was well adapted for the execution of the proposed surprise, being "deep-waisted" with a high quarter-deck, and having her guns entirely below, with no outward indication, at a distance, of either ports or armament.

On the first alarm, the hands, with one accord, had begun to swarm up on the deck, but their retirement was promptly commanded. The men required for the guns were sent to their quarters, with orders to make all ready for action, but to lift no port. The hands above, whilst requiring to move about, were kept as much as possible on the leeside of the deck, where, from the heeling of the ship and the enemy's windward position, they were in sufficient concealment. The *drummer* and *boatswain*, now most important elements in the plan, had their special instructions, whilst the crew thus became generally

sensible, by means of the orders given, of the ingenious device of their commander, so as to be well
prepared to give to it its utmost impression.

Short as the time was,—the coolness of the commander being communicated to the men, so as to
relieve the urgent haste from any embarrasing confusion,—all arrangements had been completed before
the enemy came within hailing distance. At that
period (as *apparently* from the first), everything
visible on board the Dundee indicated an unconcerned
quietness, and utter unconsciousness of danger from
the stranger's approach. The men on deck were laid
down flat on their faces. My Father coolly walking
the quarter-deck, and the helmsman engaged in his
office of steering, were the only living beings who
could be discerned from the deck of the assailant.

Without showing any colours, in answer to our
English ensign waving at the mizen-peak, the stranger
came down to within short musket-shot distance, when
a loud and unintelligible roar of the Captain, through
his speaking-trumpet, indicated the usual demand of
the nation or denomination of our ship. A significant
wave of my Father's hand served instead of a reply.
The drum beats to quarters, and whilst the roll yet
reverberates around, the shrill sound of the boatswain's pipe is heard above all. And whilst the
hoarse voice of this officer is yet giving forth the
consequent orders, the apparently plain sides of the
ship become suddenly pierced; six ports on a side
are simultaneously raised, and as many untompioned

cannon, threatening a more serious bellowing than that of the now astonished Captain's trumpet-aided voice, are run out, pointing ominously toward the enemy's broadside!

The stratagem was complete; its impression quite perfect. The adversary seemed electrified. Men on the enemy's deck, some with lighted matches in hand, and plainly visible to us by reason of her heeling position whilst descending obliquely from the windward, were seen to fall flat, as if prostrated by our shot; the guns, pointed threateningly at us, remained silent; the helm flew to port, and the yards to the wind, on our opposite tack; and without waiting for answer to his summons, or venturing to renew his attempt on such a formidable looking opponent, he suddenly hauled off, under full sail, in a direction differing, by some six points, from that in which he had previously intercepted our track!

SECTION VI.—*Extraordinary Exploit in "cutting-in," single-handed, a moderately-grown Young Whale.*

THE tardy formality with which the "flensing" of the whale was accomplished, irrespective of the particular magnitude of the animal to be despoiled of its blubber and whalebone, was frequently a source of great annoyance to my Father. The number of cuts, with the placing of straps, and attachment of tackles, had become—like the skeleton forms issued by public offices—an established system; and, cumbrous as it

was, with respect to fish of smaller growth, it was
made generally applicable to all. The effect of this
was, that whilst the largest sized fish would be flensed
in about four hours, the taking in of one of the fourth
or sixth part its size would occupy nearly half as
much time. An hour and a half at least, but more
frequently two hours, at that period of the fishery,
would be expended upon one of the ordinary small-
sized whales. The poor little carcass, indeed, was encumbered by the number of the harponeers (to whose
province belongs the fixing of the tackles and the
cutting away of the blubber) congregated upon, or
about it, whilst flensing.

As every instance of remonstrance, whilst failing
in producing any improvement, regularly induced
unpleasantness of feeling, my Father was at length
provoked to put forth a challenge, to which his
officers were able to offer no possible objection,
except the indication, by look and gesture, that
they would derive some recompense for the rebukes
passed on them, by certain and signal failure. His
adventurous challenge was, that, with the assistance
of only one-third part of the available crew, he
would go on a fish, and send it in, single-handed,
in *half the time* occupied by the four or six harponeers with the help of all hands !

Opportunities for the experiment being at this time
abundantly afforded, he forthwith prepared himself
for this trial of skill. The available hands—that is,
excluding cook, steward, surgeon, etc.—were usually

about forty-five or forty-six in number. Out of these he took, not a picked set, but only two boats' crews, with their supernumeraries, according to their existing classification, comprising about sixteen men. These he appointed to their several stations about the deck; eight to the capstan, four, perhaps, to the "crab" or "winch," and the rest to manage the "tackle-falls," to cut up the blubber and heave it into the "flens-gut," or receptacle for it below. The two boys who were appointed, on the usual plan, to hold the boat in which he was to stand whilst flensing, were, perhaps, extra; but this I forget.

Previous to the commencement of the experiment, the preparing of his cutting instruments, viz. a "blubber-spade" and "blubber-knife," became matter of personal and special attention. The *spade*, (an instrument with the cutting part about eight inches broad, and used in the manner of the "hay-spade,") was not merely ground to a fine edge and then sharpened with an oil-stone, but the sides (ordinarily left black with varnish, or encrusted with rust,) were reduced by the grindstone to a bright and smooth surface. His blubber-knife (an instrument with a three feet blade and three feet straight handle) was, in like manner, carefully ground, sharpened, and polished; so that these instruments, presenting the least possible resistance, from the adhesion of the metal to the blubber, when in use, the muscular strength of the flenser might, in no respect, be use-lessly expended.

All things being ready, and the men duly distributed, the time was noted, and my Father, single-handed, as I have said,—except as to a man to put in the straps* and attach the tackles, that he might not have occasion to wet or grease his hands,—proceeded to the trial on his apparently presumptuous challenge.

The plan he had previously determined on, and which subsequently became very common in the flensing of small fish, was the following:—

The under part of the head (always being placed upward for flensing), with the jaw-bones, "lips," and tongue, is first attached to the capstan tackle, and, being separated as it is hove up, is taken on deck altogether. Meanwhile the skull, with the whalebone and upper part of the head,—which is brought in sight, clear of the water, by the strain hove upon the other section or lower jaw,—is secured by the second tackle, and speedily made to follow its companion in the ascent to the deck.

* *Blubber-straps* are usually made out of whale-line, but some of thicker cordage, and consist of a length of about two fathoms for each strap, the ends of which being spliced together, constitute a flexible ring of rope. A hole being cut through the commencing end of the slip of blubber to be raised, the strap, being of course double, is inserted therein, and the two ends, brought together from the opposite sides of the blubber, are looped over the hook of the tackle, and so the attachment for heaving up made complete. It may here be added, that the tackles for flensing are fixed aloft to a strong rope, along which the blocks are distributed, extending (but not very tightly stretched) from the mainmast-head to that of the foremast, called the *guy*. The considerable height of this attachment of the tackles (or, technically, "speck-tackles") permits a long slip of blubber to be hove up in continuity, whilst the distribution of the blocks thereon admits of the two tackles being worked either jointly or separately without interference.

One of the fins, having a strap previously put round it, is next hove upon, till (the fish being free to roll over, so as to adjust its position to the direction of the strain,) it is well raised upward, and, the blubber annexed to it, put upon the stretch.   The fin is then easily "unsocketed," and the blubber on the seaward side being cut across beyond it, it becomes the attachment for heaving up a long slip of three or four feet in width, and extending, with its upper part, high above the level of the deck.   As this ascends, (the fish meanwhile spontaneously "canting" outwardly from the ship), the other fin appears in sight, and, being embraced by another strap, is, in its turn, hove up by the "fore-tackle" correspondently, as to its further progress, with its fellow.   When the attachment of the second, or fore-tackle, rises to about the level of the deck, the blubber-slip is cut across, just above the place of that attachment, and the separated portion, being lowered down upon the deck, is cut up, with singular celerity, into square lumps, adapted for being easily thrown about by the "pick-haak" men; and these, as rapidly as they are cut out, are made to disappear through a hole in one of the main-hatches into the flens-gut below.

The moment the first, or "after-tackle," is released, it is overhauled again over the ship's side, and, a fresh strap being fixed in the continuous slip, (which, to preserve its continuity, is cut spirally from the carcass,) the progress of the operation goes on, without ceasing, till the whole superficies of blubber is removed.

The progress in the case referred to must, doubtless, have been regarded with strange feelings of
astonishment and mortification by the severely rebuked harponeers; for, on the completion of the
operation, the watch being again appealed to, the
adventurous challenge was found to have been
triumphantly vindicated. Instead of the work being
effected, as challenged to be done, in half the time
which had been expended by thrice the force in the
number of men, it was found to have occupied but
little more than a third part of that interval. With
all hands to help, the time frequently expended by
the harponeers in flensing a small fish had been
nearly two hours ; my Father, with a third part of
the crew, had, single-handed, done the same thing in
almost forty minutes!

This extraordinary feat of tact and strength was
first accomplished, I believe, during my Father's
command of the Dundee; but the feat was repeated,
under my own observation, on board the Resolution,
and the tardiness of a burdensome system, still too
prevalently acted upon by the officers, was similarly
rebuked. To the extent, at least of a saving of
one-half the time spent in the operation by the harponeers, the bold experiment, single-handed and
with but one-third of the crew, was successfully
repeated.

My Father's plan of proceeding, in this extraordinary feat, is worthy of notice. His constitutional

habit, as I may term it, of a sort of *deliberate celerity*
was here the characteristic of his progress.   But no
time was wasted.   As fast as the men on deck could
heave-up the blubber, the blubber was freed to their
hands.   Every change of tackle, or place of working,
was so managed as to leave no interruption in the
labours of his men.   As he never himself ceased
working, he took care by judicious preconsideration,
that they should never stand idle.   On the contrary,
he had his own part always in advance of their
province, so that, in order to keep pace with him,
they were stimulated to the utmost practicable degree
of activity.   The capstan, whilst the tackle was slack,
or the strain slight, actually spun round, whilst the
hands on it, "shortening in on the bars," ran at their
utmost speed.   An instinctive spirit was infused into
every department; for no section of the men liked to
be behind, so as to be in the humiliating position of
hinderers of the others.

Though the master-hand was accomplishing so much
in so short a time,—more, in this species of work, I
may be bold to say, than any other man ever did
before or since,—there was no appearance of hurry.
His sharp and finely-polished *spade* with which he
chiefly worked, seemed to meet with no resistance
from the animal textures against which its edge was
directed.   Instead of cutting downward through the
blubber a spade-breadth at a time, as most usually
was done, he would run the instrument in a direction
obliquely horizontal, so as to separate the slip then

heaving up from the general envelopment of the blubber, for a yard or two in extent, at a single stroke or thrust of the instrument. The slight attachment of the blubber to the muscles of the carcass could then be usually torn away (with a touch underneath with the spade when incidentally needful to be cut) by the force with which the slip was being raised by the mechanical engines in motion on the deck.

Thus proceeding with calm and quiet self-possession, and with unceasing perseverance, few cuts being made but at the best advantage, and no stroke of his cutting-tools being struck in vain, the work proceeded with such despatch as to accomplish the extraordinary results we have just described.

CHAPTER IV.

THE SHIP " RESOLUTION," OF WHITBY.

SECTION I.—*Continued Prosperity:—the Results,
comparatively and generally, of this
fresh Enterprise.*

THE change of command which, in the progress of
our Memorials, comes now under consideration, was
brought about by two circumstances;—the great inconvenience of a family residence at Whitby, whilst
my Father was sailing from, and returning to, London; and the incidental formation of a co-partnery
at Whitby, which my Father was invited to join, for
the building and equipment of a new Greenland ship
from that port.

The advantages, in point of comfort and convenience alone, were such as to render the change in
ship and port to which this scheme pointed, highly
desirable; and most earnestly and imploringly was
the proposition of the parties at Whitby supported
by my long discomforted and pining mother. But
the conditions submitted to my Father were equally
acceptable. It was designed that the co-partnery
should consist of the holders of eight equal shares,
of 1000*l.* each; that Messrs. Fishburn and Brodrick,
the designed builders of the ship, should hold two

shares, five other inhabitants of Whitby, as arranged among themselves, each a share, making seven, and my Father the eighth. His wages and perquisites, too, on the liberal and advanced scale as allowed him by the Messrs. Gale, were to be continued.

Without difficulty, and with but little loss of time, the arrangements were all completed, and the owners of the Dundee, who were justly esteemed for their honourable and generous dealing by their Captain, had due and respectful notice given them of the intended change, and were easily made sensible of the propriety of it, as far as regarded his personal well-being.

In the " Resolution," a fine, substantial, and in all respects well-built ship of 291 tons burden, was comprised the property of the new co-partnery. The cost of the ship, with casks and all other stores, was 6321*l*. 3*s*. 4*d*. The provisions for the voyage, together with insurance, and the advance wages usually paid to the men, amounted to 1470*l*. 4*s*. 1*d*. Thus the total expenditure in preparation for the voyage was 7791*l*. 7*s*. 5*d*., leaving a small balance out of the sum subscribed in the hands of the managers.

The proceedings on board the ship, with the results of this adventure, for, and during the whole time of my Father's command (a period of eight years), are in considerable detail before me, being comprised in a regular series of journals kept by myself. For young as I was when the Resolution commenced her career of adventure—being then but thirteen—I was

regularly installed, and by no means unwillingly, in
training for the whale-fishery as a profession, as one
of her apprenticed hands.

On the 21st of February, 1803, the ship was
launched, and duly " christened" the "Resolution;"
and on the 21st of March, she left her moorings in
the harbour and proceeded to sea. We made the
ice on the 2d of April; on the 12th were in latitude
78° 40′ N. in sight of the "Middle Hook of the
Foreland;" and on the 18th "struck" and killed our
first whale. The 20th was a prosperous day, for so
early a period of the season, adding two more large
fish to our commencing cargo. The 29th, however,
was very different, being a day of mortifying adventure. We had obtained shelter, during a gale of
wind, under the lee-side of a "field,"—a large and
continuous sheet of ice extending beyond the reach
of vision from the mast-head,—where several whales,
(chiefly old ones, with their cubs or calves,) were
met with. Four of them—comprising two old and
two cubs — were harpooned during the day. The
little ones, of but trifling value, were captured; but
both the "mothers" escaped. One of them had been
so energetically assailed as to receive four harpoons,—
a condition from which the capture generally results,
—when she made a most determinate advance beneath
and beyond the ice. She ultimately escaped, carrying away with her a spoil (a painful and deadly boon,
indeed, to herself) of a harpoon, with twelve attached
lines, comprising a total extent of 1440 fathoms, or

about a mile and two-thirds, in measure ! The next day, however, yielded us some compensation, in the capture of another *large* fish, a result altogether not a little inspiriting, where the attainment of an amount of six whales, before the expiration of the month of April, was a circumstance rarely, if ever, realized before. Our thirteenth fish was killed on the 8th of June ; but, though we persevered about ten days longer, and had well nigh captured another fish, in which two harpoons were struck, we made no accession to our not full, but, as the season went, most satisfactory cargo.

In looking over my journal for materials for this abstract, it was singularly interesting and pleasant to the feelings to find, under date of the 27th of June, when the good ship Resolution was on her homeward passage, a written recognition, which I remember to have received from my Father, of the Divine hand and Providence in respect of the successes obtained. It is comprised in this brief but appropriate Collect:— " O most merciful Father, who of Thy gracious goodness hast crowned our labours with success, we give Thee humble and hearty thanks for this, Thy special bounty, beseeching Thee to continue Thy loving kindness unto us, that we may enjoy the fruits of our labours to Thy glory and our comfort, through Jesus Christ our Lord, Amen."

The proceeds of this first voyage in oil were $163\frac{1}{2}$ tuns: the *Whitby* average of the same year (exclusive of the Resolution's cargo) being only 62 tuns,

and the greatest catch among the rest of the Whitby
fleet being eight whales, yielding 139 tuns of oil.
Hence, with relation to the average of the port,—
six ships,—my Father's success stood in the ratio of
2·8 to 1, or nearly three to one!

But subsequent voyages—the next three especially
—proved regularly and increasingly prosperous; the
cargoes of the years 1804, 1805, and 1806, yielding
a produce of rather more than 600 tuns of oil, derived from the capture of eighty-seven whales. The
entire proceeds of my Father's enterprises in eight
voyages, in this successful ship, amounted to 194
whales, yielding 1617 tuns of oil, or an average of
twenty-four whales and one-fourth, with 202 tuns of
oil per voyage!

His competitors from the same port, during the
whole of this particular period, comprising 7·8 ships
a year, obtained, on the eight years' average, only
sixty-eight fish, yielding 646·4 tuns of oil ; whilst the
united cargoes of the most successful ship of each
year, amounted but to 138 whales, 1228 tuns of oil;
this select amount being exceeded by nearly a third
part, by my Father's individual catch; and the general
average being exceeded in the proportion of two and
a half to one!

But it was hardly to be expected that, whatever
might be my Father's peculiar superiority, as compared with the general body of competitors, no one,
out of many hundreds of different commanders,
should be found successfully to emulate, within a

long series of years, even his extraordinary enterprise.

Yet, closely as two or three individuals commanding
in the Greenland fishery might approximate, or occasionally exceed, his successes, it is remarkable that
no one, within any of the periods of the Henrietta,
the Dundee, or the Resolution, or within the whole
period of nineteen years, ever went beyond him!

My Father's most successful competitor, within
the longest period of cotemporary enterprise, ending
with the year 1810, was Mr. Angus Sadler, of Hull.
From 1796 to 1810 (fifteen voyages) they fished in
the same region, the Greenland Seas, my Father
obtaining 2693 tuns of oil, and Mr. Sadler 2539.
In the eight voyages of the Resolution, however, the
competition was singularly close; Mr. Sadler bringing
home the produce of only two whales in number
less, and the exact same quantity (1617 tuns) of oil.
But, in this comparison, my Father was at great disadvantage from the inferior size of his ship,—the
Aurora, of Hull, which Mr. Sadler commanded in
several of his most prosperous voyages, being of the
burden of 366 tons, and the Resolution only of 291.
This difference of capacity was very important,
enabling Mr. Sadler, in two or three different voyages,
to bring home a quantity of produce exceeding by
some sixty or seventy tuns, altogether, the capabilities
of stowage of the Resolution,—which ship, five years
out of eight, having been what was called "a full
ship," might, no doubt, have obtained some greater

G

cargoes, and, by consequence, a better position in the competition, had her capacity been larger.

It falls not within my present province, nor within the scope of my materials, to set forth the considerable successes of some other leading fishermen at the time of the Resolution's enterprises. I may merely notice, that Mr. Kearsley, of the Henrietta (trained under my Father), was the most successful of the other *Whitby* captains; and that some enterprising men, commanding ships out of *Scotland*, began now, or soon after this, to take a high position in the prosperous class.

The only other *general* competitor of my Father's yet to be named, whose enterprises were cotemporary during the whole or greater part of his career, from 1792 to 1810, was Captain John Marshall, of Hull. Within the *western* field of Arctic enterprise—the whale-fishery of *Davis' Strait*—Captain Marshall stood pre-eminent. His successes there corresponded very much with those of my Father in the fishery of Greenland; and the total results did not materially differ. Whilst my Father's successes yielded, within the period referred to 2728 tuns of oil, Captain Marshall's, though deprived of the chance of one year's adventure in which he remained on shore, amounted to 2691 tuns. Had the full nineteen years been completed, his successes would, probably, have been the greatest. But the *services*, and the qualities required for them, differ so materially, as not to permit, in fairness, of an arithmetical comparison

of the *mere quantities* of produce. For success in
the fishery of Davis' Strait, at the time under consideration, was a far more easy undertaking than in
that of Greenland. This fact is satisfactorily derived
from a comparison of the average success in the two
fisheries. In seventeen years out of the nineteen
under review, (there being no ship from Hull to
Davis' Strait during 1792 and 1793,) the average
success of 313 Greenland whalers from Hull was
a produce in oil of 84·4 tuns, whilst the mean success of the Davis' Strait fishery, 190 ships, was for
the same period 124·3,—indicating, most clearly, that
the latter fishery then afforded a better chance of a
cargo than the fishery of Greenland, in the ratio of
very nearly three to two !*

Hence, my Father's success, when taken on the
most extensive comparison with the fishermen of his
day, stands decidedly conspicuous and pre-eminent.
And this pre-eminence, it should be noted, was not only
in the amount of the cargoes he obtained, but also in
the shortness of the time occupied in his voyages; for
whilst the general average of Greenland voyages of
this period (as indicated, at least, by the extensive
enterprise from the port of Hull,) comprised four
months and nineteen days, the average of my Father's
absence from sailing to his return was, in the Reso-

---

* The proportion of profit, it may be noted, did not equal that of the
relative produce obtained from the two fisheries, in consequence of the
additional expenses of the Davis' Strait voyage, in respect of the time
absent, and of the higher premium required for insurance.

lution's eight voyages, only three months and twenty-
eight days!

It may not be uninteresting to some of our readers
to be informed, before we conclude this section of
results, of the actual realization in gross amount of
value, and in profits divided amongst the partners, in
this prosperous whale-fishing adventure. This, by
reason of a complete abstract of the payments and
receipts during the greater part of the Resolution's
career, I am enabled to give with perfect accuracy:—

PAYMENTS.

	£	s.	d.
Expenses on First Voyage, including Outfit of the Second	4008	18	4
Ditto for Second Voyage	4476	2	6
Ditto for Third Voyage	4679	11	5
Ditto on Fourth and Fifth . . .	9216	14	6
Ditto on Sixth	5823	14	4
Ditto on Seventh	4729	11	8
Ditto on Eighth	4722	11	5
	£ 37,657	4	2

RECEIPTS.

	£	s.	d.
Proceeds of Cargo and Government Bounty (20s. per ton on the ship's measurement, or 291l.) on the First Voyage .	6864	10	5
Ditto, Second Voyage . . .	6568	1	0
Ditto, Third	6287	10	9
Ditto, Fourth and Fifth . . .	10,428	7	11
Ditto, Sixth	7157	8	6
Ditto, Seventh	8275	14	6
Ditto, Eighth	8195	16	10
Amount of Receipts	£ 53,777	9	11
Ditto Expenses	37,657	4	2
Clear Profits	£ 16,120	5	9

This balance I have stated as "clear profits," because, in consequence of the perfect state of repair of
the Resolution, the large augmentation in the quantity of her stores, and the increased cost of shipping,
the value of the ship (augmented by the charge of
outfit for the ninth voyage in the table of expenses)
was scarcely at all deteriorated.   Hence we derive
for the clear profit on the original advance of 8000*l.*,
—a capital still existing,—during eight years continuously, the sum of 2015*l.* 0*s.* 8*d.* a year, or 25 per
cent per annum.

With this result, the enterprises of my Father in
the Resolution, of Whitby (influenced, in a considerable degree, I believe, by a kindly and parental consideration for myself), concluded.   For on the very
day on which I completed my twenty-first year, he,
at a Board of the co-partnery, specially summoned,
formally resigned his command; and, on the same
day,—the earliest at which, by reason of age, I could
legally hold a command,—I was unanimously elected
his successor.

Whilst thus retiring from the command of the
Resolution, my Father was by no means disposed to
abandon his stirring and highly remunerative occupation.   At the very period of his retirement, indeed,
the opportunity of a new and satisfactory connection
was, incidentally by my own medium, opened to
him, of which he forthwith availed himself.

But before entering on the relation of his subsequent enterprises, we shall proceed, according to our usual plan, to adduce a few incidents or circumstances, illustrative, mainly, of character or talents, which are associated with this period of our memorial history.

SECTION II.—*Treatment and Recovery of a half-frozen Seaman.*

THE peculiarity of the conflicts, and the severity of the climate, encountered by the Arctic whale-fishers, yield a characteristic novelty both to the incidents and accidents of their adventure. So that, although the incidents of whaling enterprise may, for the most part, possess such general characteristics as to admit of some classification among themselves, they are at the same time novel, when considered in relation to the results of ordinary adventure; whilst, every now and then, an accident happens, or a circumstance is met with, which, taken on the broadest scheme of comparison, is found to be *sui generis.*

Such incidents afford special occasions for the exercise of inherent science and originality of intellect in those who have to deal with the results. And, I may add, every accident or occurrence of this kind, which claimed my Father's directing consideration, was, in all cases that I ever heard of, dealt with in a manner consistent with a condition of mind of inexhaustible resources in itself.

Several cases of this description happened, whilst I was myself present, during my youthful training as a seaman and a fisherman. The one referred to, in the title of this section, was specially interesting.

Whilst the ship Resolution navigated an open lake of water, in the 81st degree of latitude,—something like the Baltic Sea in magnitude,—during a keen frost and strong northerly wind, a whale appeared, and a boat put off in pursuit.* On its second visit to the surface the boat came up with it, and a harpoon was securely struck. A convulsive and terrible heave of its ponderous tail, which succeeded the wound, struck the boat at the stern, and by its reaction projected the boat-steerer overboard. As the line attached to the harpoon drew the boat instantly off, the crew threw some of their oars towards him for his support, one of which he fortunately seized.

The auxiliary boats, as well as the ship, being at a considerable distance, and the fast-boat being rapidly drawn away from the imperilled seaman, the harpooneer, under the instinctive impulse of humanity, cut his line with the view of yielding him succour. But no sooner was the sacrifice made than, to the great mortification of all in the boat, it was found to be useless; for, in consequence of the loss of oars, some being thrown towards the sufferer, and some broken or carried off by the stroke from the whale, the boat had become altogether unmanageable!

A considerable time elapsed before the headmost auxiliary boat reached the place: happily they were so far in time that the object of their anxious solicitude

* Given in substance in the "Account of the Arctic Regions," vol. ii. page 360.

still floated, stretched over an oar, whilst retaining but little sensation.

On his arrival at the ship, being hauled up the side by ropes, with judicious help from his comrades in the boat, he was found to be in a deplorable condition. His clothes were frozen like a casing of mail, and his hair was consolidated into a helmet of ice.

My Father, having ordered him to be taken into the cabin abaft, gave his immediate attention, in guidance and precedence of the ship's surgeon, in a system of treatment which, under the circumstances, was, perhaps, the most judicious that could have been adopted.

Whilst placed on the cabin floor, where the temperature was moderate, but not high, the frozen clothing of the patient was forthwith removed, and his person dried with warm towels, and then industriously rubbed, by two or three hands at a time, with well heated coarse cloths and flannels. There being great exhaustion, and all but a suspension of the circulation, stimulating cordial was administered as he was able to take it.

When the process of friction had been continued until sensation began to be restored, and the general faculties in some measure awakened, he was covered with dry under clothing, and placed, amid an abundance of warm blankets, in my Father's bed. After a few hours' sleep he awoke considerably resuscitated, but complained of a painful sensation of cold.

Some warm and nourishing diluents having been given to him, he was conducted to his own berth, and, with the view of removing his distressing feeling of chilliness, two of his comrades were requested to accompany him; where, one on each side, their abundant healthful circulation and animal heat, proved most effective in ministering, restoratively, to these defects in the condition of the patient.

The shock on his constitution, however, was greater, with respect to his apparent early recovery, than was anticipated. He was so far restored, within a few days, as to be able to engage in his usual duties; but months elapsed before his countenance exhibited its wonted glow and appearance of health.

SECTION III.—*Judicious Treatment of Men having suffered from severe Exposure.*

THE Resolution was moored to a flat sheet of ice, surrounded by streams and open drift ice, on the 30th of April, 1808. It blew fresh, and the weather was cold. In the evening a whale was harpooned, which ran out about the length of a mile and a half of line from the fast-boat. Other harpoons, and several lances, were then struck, and no doubt remained with the pursuers but that it would speedily become their prize. But this expectation signally failed. A tremendous and convulsive throe of the whale produced an extraordinary effect: one of the lines, and also a harpoon were broken, and the other two harpoons

G 2

drawn out simultaneously, when, to the astonishment of the beholders, the imagined capture was found, in one moment, to have become free. It dived and escaped!

A storm meanwhile had commenced. Five boats, with their crews, remained for the getting in of the long length of line run out from the first fast-boat, whilst two, myself in one of them, returned to the ship, in aid of the inadequate residue of men—for any nautical operation—left on board.

Thick snow set in, the storm increased, and the ship, being fast to a *light* piece of ice, drifted rapidly to leeward, and away from the boats. We became distressfully anxious about the safety of the absent men. At one the next morning the mooring was cut, and the ship being got under way, was worked on short tacks to windward, in the supposed direction of the boats. At three we were rejoiced by the appearance of three of the boats, which, with crews unharmed, we got safely on board. The remainder, they reported, might be expected by the same track in half an hour.

Cheered by this hope, we continued making every effort to get the ship to windward. But, long after the time of their expected return, no other boat appeared. Hour after hour of anxiety and distress passed over whilst we navigated, off and on, among troublesome and dangerous ices. Guns were fired occasionally, and at every unoccupied interval all hands were engaged in the one object which sym-

pathy urged—the straining of their eyes in the hope
of discerning the boats of their comrades through
the obscurity of the snow. The obscurity was not
attenuated; the storm raged, and the sea increased,
whilst a foreboding gloom appeared in every countenance, darkening and keeping pace with the dis-
malness of the night. The loss of one-half of the
Ipswich's crew on a similar occasion was yet fresh on
our minds, and low whisperings of expressions of
fear, and shuddering responses, indicated a prevailing dread of a similar fate to their comrades.

At length, happy moment! a little after eight in
the morning, a sudden shout of joy announced the
discovery of the boats, and in a few minutes we had
the undescribable satisfaction of seeing them alongside. Aided by those on board with ropes and hands,
they were all, twelve to fourteen in number, received
safe on board, and welcomed with the most heartfelt
greeting by their truly exulting shipmates.

The natural desire and effort to get below, into a
place of genial warmth, both with the shivering
sailors and the sympathising people on board, was,
with most judicious consideration on the part of my
Father, restrained. The men had been suffering from
more than a twelve hours' exposure, without food or
adequate extra clothing, to cold and storm,—the thermometer, which had been as low as 13 degrees, being still
8 or 10 degrees below freezing,—and many were partially frost-bitten, and some stiff and half-paralyzed
with the severity of the weather. In this case, he wisely

considered, that sudden transition to the warm gal-
ley, and proximity to the blazing fire of the cabouse
below, might be productive of dangerous, possibly of
fatal, effects. He felt it was needful for their safety
that means should be *previously* adopted for restoring,
in some measure, the arrested or retarded circulation.

Stimulants, in a case of this kind, moderately administered, were considered advantageous ; but friction,
and muscular exercise, much more essential to safety.
Those, therefore, whose hands or feet, or faces or
ears, had become *white* (like the appearance of a
tallow candle) by the utter abstraction of the blood,
had their frost-bitten parts actively and perseveringly
rubbed with the open hands of others, and the worst
cases with snow, until the endurance of the severe,
or even agonizing pain usually attending the recovery, when the repelled circulation begins to be
restored in the affected parts, had removed the risk
of *mortification* taking place. Others were variously
exercised, as they were able to make muscular efforts
of themselves, or with the assistance of others. Those
who were capable of the exertion were made to run
about the deck, chasing, or being chased, one by
another. And soon apprehending, as most of them
did, the wisdom of the measures adopted, they not
only entered into them heartily, but those who had
been the most affected, as soon as their limbs obtained
power for the exertion, were ready to join, or to
attempt to join, in the exercise and race, until some
glow of warmth, and consciousness of restored sensa-

tion, had taken place of the pre-existing chilliness or insensibility. They were then, under strict cautions against approaching at first too near the fire, suffered to go below; and, happily, under this wise and effective treatment, all escaped without any permanent injury.

A stout Shetland boy had well nigh fallen a sacrifice to the severity of the exposure. He expressed a great desire, whilst abroad in one of the boats, for sleep, and earnestly entreated the men, who objected to the indulgence of the inclination, to allow him to compose himself for half an hour, " for he was sure," he said, " that he should dream of the situation of the ship." After a few minutes' repose, which they were induced to permit, he was awoke, but with difficulty, and it required considerable attention on the part of his companions to keep him from a sleep which, under such circumstances, they well knew must be the harbinger of death.

Other instances of the happy exercise of good judgment in the treatment of men who had suffered long exposure to cold and hunger, might have been adduced had I particularly noted them. One other case, though of no real danger, (occurring May 29th, 1809,) may be briefly mentioned, in which I was personally a participator.

It was blowing a fresh gale from the north-east, with strong frost, thermometer 20°, but the sea was not very considerable because of the sheltering in-

fluence of surrounding ice. Two whales were captured; but one of them dying at a great depth under
water, had to be hauled up by the united crews of
two or three boats, which proved a tedious and severe
labour. We were absent from the ship from fourteen to sixteen hours, without food or shelter from
the inclement gale, sometimes lying inertly on our
oars waiting for the rising of the harpooned whales,
or for the hauling up of the sunken one to the surface; and sometimes we were engaged in pulling
about, hauling in lines, or in "towing" the dead
fish to the ship. By the time we got on board we
were mostly in a state of considerable exhaustion, and
all were painfully suffering from cold and hunger.

My Father had considerately provided for our
return. Instead of the distribution of ardent spirits,
—the measure universally resorted to at this period,
with the view of cheering and restoring the depressed
energies of any long-exposed party of adventurers in
the boats,—a far better and more effective provision
had been made. A huge kettle of coffee was boiling
on the fire, which, with the usual supplies of bread
and beef, was distributed in ample quantity among
the half-starved party now returning; and a more
grateful or more salutary instance of administered refreshment I do not remember ever to have enjoyed.
The heat of this beverage, supplied as it was so
liberally to all, had the most happy effect in aiding
the restoration of the animal heat, and of exhilarating
without unduly stimulating the depressed physical

condition of the men. The case afforded an admirable practical example of the correctness of the
principles generally asserted, in favour of simple
drinks over spirituous or fermented stimulants, by
the advocates of " Temperance."

SECTION IV.—*The Crow's Nest.*

THE invention of the CROW'S NEST in the form
now universally used by the British Arctic whalers,
and adopted generally by our discovery ships, deserves, from its convenience, comfort, and importance, a special record.

For the safe and effective navigation of the Arctic
ices, as well as for a due watch being kept for the
discovery of whales, an elevated position on the
mast, as a station for the directing or "look-out"
officer, is absolutely necessary. In seas covered over
with numerous masses of ice, or in positions where
the navigation is at once encumbered, difficult, and
perhaps dangerous, it is impossible for the officer
on deck to perform the duty, at all adequately, of
directing the ship's course and progress.

From time immemorial, therefore, the captains of
whalers, or other acting officers, have always been
wont to take their station occasionally, and when
necessity required, at the mast-head, or rather on
the main top-mast "cross-trees." For the benefit
of a little shelter from the piercing breezes in this
exposed situation, some ships were provided with a

canvas screen of about three and a half or four feet
in height, passed round the sides and fore-part of
the top-gallant rigging, from the top-mast cross-trees
upward. This, with a sort of wooden rail for a seat,
extending betwixt the aftermost shrouds of the top-
gallant rigging, afforded the *best crow's nest* hitherto
made use of; a shelter tolerably effective when the
ship was sailing by or near the wind, but altogether
useless when going with the wind abaft the beam.
It was not very safe either, as accidents from sleepi-
ness, or the giving way of the very inadequate seat,
sometimes happened. Besides, when top-gallant sails
were set, this contrivance was all but useless. But
a far inferior sort of protection than this was in frequent or ordinary use at the time of my first experience in the Arctic seas. For years, I remember,
we had nothing more for sheltering behind but bits
of canvas on either side of the top-gallant rigging
and round the top-mast head, without anything in
front; and in some voyages still less,—a slip of canvas bound round the head of the top-mast and heel
of the top-gallant mast, spreading some eighteen
inches to two feet wide, and perhaps three and a
half feet high, being all that the poor officer had to
shield him from the most penetrating severity of the
Arctic winds. Often have I myself sat, when a little
boy, by the side of my Father for hours at a time, in
this wretchedly exposed position, shivering with cold
generally, and with hands and feet frequently in
severe pain, whilst he habituated me in his superior
practice of navigating amid dangerous ices.

The consequences of this deficiency of protection were,—that the proper navigation of the ship was often neglected, the discovery of many whales sufficiently within view from thence was prevented, and the success of the adventure was much restricted.

The greatest boon, therefore, of modern times, ever given to the Arctic navigator, it may be safely, I think, said, was my Father's invention of the *round top-gallant crow's nest.* It was in May, 1807, I believe, in which the first of these was built. It was placed, in the first instance, at the top-mast head, but ultimately, when the invention became perfected, it was perched, like a rostrum, on the head of the main top-gallant mast, with nothing whatever above.

This structure, as most approved by the inventor, is about four and a half feet in height and two and a half in diameter. The form is cylindrical, open above and closed below. The frame-work of the cylindrical part is covered with leather or canvas. The entrance is by a trap-hatch at the bottom. Arrangements are made for the depositing (sheltered from the weather) of various pieces of useful apparatus, such as speaking-trumpet, telescope, signal-flag, perhaps a rifle for shooting narwals, compass, etc. For the more effectual shelter of the observer when standing up, a moveable screen, two or three feet wide and adding a foot to the elevation, is placed on the windward side, and shifted whenever the ship is tacked, or the course materially changed.

The protection thus obtained from the chilling action of the wind is most perfect. Not a breath of air stirs within this elevated rostrum. The observer has free use of all his limbs, and, being safe from the possibility of falling, has nothing to disturb him in giving his entire attention to the navigation of the ship and the look-out for whales. Being perched, too, on the most elevated part of the mast, there is nothing to interfere with his view of the whole area of the circle of vision, having, in clear weather, a diameter of twenty to twenty-two geographical miles. So supported, and so effectually protected, with the means of sitting, and space for moving about when standing, there is no particular hardship, in tolerable weather, in remaining at the mast-head for some hours together. Often has this elevated position been occupied by my Father, (and often by myself, too,) during ten or twelve hours, and sometimes fourteen hours or more, within the twenty-four.

This invention has not only added unspeakably to the comfort and security of the officer at the mast-head, but has, no doubt, contributed greatly both to the safety of ships navigating the Arctic ices, and, in respect of its position for " a good look-out," in no inconsiderable degree to the prosperity of their adventures.

The attainment of this position during storm and snow, or when the rigging, as not unfrequently happens, is covered with glassy ice, is the chief matter

of discomfort, difficulty, and risk.   The frigid northerly blast feels as if blowing quite through and
through you.   The ascent, by the ordinary rigging
and ratlings, conducts you to about three-fourths of
the elevation of the top-mast; you then step into midships, upon a series of battens extending betwixt the
top-mast backstays; and, finally, when approaching
the cross-trees, you proceed up a vertically stretched
ladder of ropes and battens,—ropes on the sides, and
battens as steps,—until you make lodgment within the
crow's nest by the trap-hatch, which, being then put
down, forms a part of the close and secure platform.

Section V.—*Extraordinary Celerity in preparing
an empty Boat for active Service in the Fishery.*

In the celerity with which he accomplished com-
plex or tedious operations pertaining to seamanship
or the whale-fishery, my Father stood quite unrivalled.
We have elucidated this characteristic in a former
section, in respect to the flensing of a young whale
with extraordinary rapidity, and we now adduce
another example of a more incidental nature.

During the outward passage towards the fishing-
stations, the boats, designed for the fishery, are
carried out in an entirely dismantled state,—some
being stowed away upon deck, and some, perhaps,
below.   On reaching the ice it is usual to suspend a
couple of boats, or more, by their davits, at the
quarters of the ship, to be ready for sealing, or any

occasional purpose. But the whale-lines and other fishing apparatus are not wont to be put into them until the ship reaches, or approaches near to, some of the accustomed fishing-stations.

The boats of the Resolution were in this second condition on the 11th of April, 1808, when the ship, in her progress northward, had reached the 71st degree of latitude,—a parallel in which whales were not expected to be met with. It happened, however, on the occasion alluded to, (as I find it noted in my log-book, kept at the time,) that a whale made its appearance very near to the ship. It was in the morning, early, whilst my Father was yet in bed; but he was not called, because, in the unprepared condition of the boats, the officer of the watch, and indeed all the people on deck, considered the pursuit of it to be utterly impracticable.

My Father, however, as little trammelled in judgment by ordinary usages as he was in the habit of being guided by popular ideas of the limits of practicability, was much annoyed by the officer's assumption, which had prevented his being called. "It was no use disturbing you," the officer pleaded, "as there was not a boat in readiness for the fishery." "But a boat might have been got ready," was the confidently asserted rebuke. That this could have been done, however, within the short period of time in which a solitary whale might be expected to remain within sight, seemed to the officers as utterly impossible; for whilst a whale, under such circumstances, would seldom be found to remain within sight for half an hour, the preparing of the boats with lines, harpoons, and other requisites for the fishery, would, as they conceived, occupy several hours.

My Father maintained, however, the practicability of a boat being fitted out, in a manner sufficient for efficiency, in the course of a quarter of an hour; and, when the idea was unhesitatingly objected to as an *impossibility*, he undertook to prove his assertion. A boat then hanging at the larboard quarter, empty, except as to oars, he selected for an experiment, and undertook, with the help only of the watch upon deck,—about sixteen hands,—to have that boat ready for active service within the space of fifteen minutes.

To the due apprehending of this unprecedented undertaking, it will be proper to describe what is ordinarily deemed needful for fitting out a boat for the harpooning and capturing of the whale. The loose furniture of oars, harpoons, lances, etc., present no particular difficulty; but the supplying of an adequate quantity of lines, and placing them in a condition for being safely run out, is, as ordinarily practised, a long and tedious operation. The lines, it may be mentioned, are taken on board from their winter storehouse, in coils made up by the ropemaker, in the shape of a short drum, each coil weighing a little more than a hundred-weight, and measuring 120 fathoms in length. They are so coiled, in regular layers, commencing with that of the slender square or cylindrical centre on which they are wound, that

they may be either unwound, by reversing the
original motion of the coil from the exterior, or by
taking up the inner end left loose in the open centre,
the line may be drawn out thence whilst the coil
remains at rest. For the lodgment of the lines, when
deliberately preparing for the fishery, they are *unrolled*
from the cylindrical mass, and coiled in compartments
in the boats as they come off; but as this could not
be done under a period of some hours, the running of
the lines out of the centre of the coils was the plan
alone available for my Father's object.

Whilst every article of the requisite apparatus was
yet in the place of its ordinary lodgment,—harpoons
and lances being in the places appropriated for them
in the 'tween decks, and whale-lines in the gun-
room,—the time for commencing was noted, and my
Father proceeded, as I very well recollect witnessing,
to the proof of this new feat of activity and management.

To the several hands of the "watch," now gathered
round him, was distinctly apportioned his part of
the undertaking; first of all in bringing promptly on
deck the requisite quantity of whale-lines and fishing
apparatus, and then in placing them fit for service.
Several lines (I think about four in number) were
stowed away in different compartments of the boat,
with the interior cavity of each upward. The inner
end of the line of one of the coils, in the most favourable position for running, was rapidly "spliced" to
the "foreganger" of the harpoon by my Father,

whilst the officers about him were set to the splicing properly together of the alternate outside end of one coil with the inner end of another, so as to constitute an appropriate running series. Everything being accomplished, and the boat got ready for lowering, the time was again noted, when, to the astonishment of all on board, the interval expended was found only to have been *twelve* minutes!

The rebuke of the officer of the morning watch, thus experimentally justified, occasioned, very naturally, a desire to question, if questioning could in any one particular be maintained, the effectiveness or safety of the preparations thus hastily made. And it *was* questioned whether lines so disposed, for being run off the ropemaker's coils, would be safe to trust to their running clear in the case of actual service. This matter was soon settled by a most satisfactory experiment. As a whale when harpooned does not go faster away than a man can run, it was proposed to run off the whole of the lines out of the boat by hand, in order to prove that the arrangements that had been made were adequate, both for ordinary service and safety.

The decks were forthwith cleared, fore and aft, and the men arranged to run with the line, from the boat to the forecastle, in unceasing succession,—a service which they performed, after the word was given to start, with a hearty goodwill and their utmost activity; and the experiment was admirably successful. The whole of the lines went out of the

boat, by the usual notch over the stem, without hitch
or failure of the slightest kind interrupting their free
progress from beginning to end!

SECTION VI.—*Tact and Bravery in attacking and
killing a dangerously-resisting Whale.*

IT was no uncommon event for my Father, in case
of any difficult or dangerous enterprise in the fishery,
to take part himself in the adventure. The special
case now referred to will illustrate at once his practice and talent.

On the 29th of May, 1807, a whale was harpooned
by one of our officers. It descended to some considerable depth, but speedily returned. On its re-
appearance, it evinced an uncommon degree of
irritation. Its motions, whilst making but little
progress a-head, were vehement and incessant,—
rolling itself quite over, or, in an oscillating manner,
from side to side ; throwing its huge tail into the air,
or flinging it with fearful impulse right and left, and
so keeping the surface of the sea around it in perpetual
commotion and foam. The display of its fins and tail
was so terrific and dangerous, that few of those in
command of our boats were hardy enough to approach
it. But, under this violent action of the fish, and the
inaction of our men, the risk of losing the hoped-for
prize became imminent. This being evident to my
Father, who, with discerning and watchful eye, had
all along been viewing from the masthead, with

intense anxiety, the exciting scene with his glass,—
he made the signal, and in a manner indicative of
urgent haste, for one of the boats to come to the
ship.   In brief space,—the fish not being far distant,
—he had personally embarked on his dangerous enterprise.

On reaching the scene of action, where the wounded
monster was still exerting its excited energies in
aiming blows at any approaching boats, or thrashing
the sea into a foam,—our accomplished whale-hunter
quietly assumed a station, in parallelism, nearly, with
the direction of the animal's extended length, and
within a few fathoms of its broadside.   The boat-
steerer,—as the custom is,—he guided by the motion
of his hand; but the boat's crew, being previously
urged to exert a tremendous spring on their oars
when he should decide on making his attack, were
to await his verbal command.

A favourable pause, succeeding a terrific display
of action and power, had been watchfully discerned
by my Father, when, giving the signal to the boat-
steerer to sheer towards the fish, and, simultaneously,
the emphatic order to the men,—"Give way, my
lads; give way!"—he was in a moment placed within
reach; and then, at long arm's length, whilst leaning
over the boat's bow for distance' sake, he plunged
his well-sharpened harpoon deep into the writhing
creature's side.   Its usual vengeance-slash of its tail
was made harmlessly; for the order to "back off,"
had been so instantly and effectively obeyed, that the

H

boat was beyond reach before this ponderous engine of motion or destruction could be thrown out.

Rebuked, in a measure, by this daring attack of their commander, as well as encouraged and stimulated by its success, one of the hitherto hesitating boats immediately followed for a similar object; but the officer commanding it, not having the same tact, advanced incautiously, at an unfavourable moment, and too far within the range of the enemy's destructive members, as to subject himself and comrades to a formidable peril. The tail of the fish was again reared into the air, in a terrific attitude over the boat. The harponeer, who was directly underneath, happily discovered his danger, and leaped overboard; and the next moment the threatened stroke was impressed with tremendous force upon the centre of the boat, which literally buried it in the water!

Providentially, no one was hurt. The officer who leaped overboard, escaped certain death by the prompt adventure. The huge tail (a member measuring perhaps twenty feet in width, extending to a superficial area of about eighty square feet, and weighing from one to two tons), struck the very spot on which he had previously stood. The effects of the blow on the boat were extraordinary. The keel was broken; the gunwale, and all the planks, except two, were cut through; and it was evident that the boat would have been completely divided, had not the tail struck directly upon a deep coil of the whale-lines. The crew, succoured by the various boats lying around, were all speedily picked up; but the boat was so thoroughly smashed as to be rendered useless.

This alarming discouragement, with the crippling of their strength and resources by the destruction of one boat and the withdrawal of another for the conveyance to the ship of the drenched and shivering sailors, threw the principal burden of the exploit of capture on my Father. For though other harpoons, after some minor adventures, were struck, the actual killing of this leviathan of its tribe was effected by himself.

Contrary to the usual habits of the Greenland whale, this individual, instead of occasionally seeking the depths of ocean for its protection, especially on receiving a fresh and painful wound, remained mainly at the surface. Its natural energies, but yet little acted on by the exhausting influence of the *pressure* of water, were consequently very little impaired; for the superficial wounds of harpoons produce no immediate effect upon life.

Hence, the operation of lancing was yet to be effected, before there could be any chance of subduing the still existing dangerous vigour. My Father, as was his wont, proceeded next to this venturous undertaking. Again he plants his boat in parallelism of position with that of his gigantic game. Full of ardour and confidence in their leader, his boat's crew are ready for any effort or adventure which the daring or activity of man may accomplish. The proper moment for the attack is waited for, and,

when seen, instantly improved. The boat, as a thing
of life, springs, at his signal, towards the side of the
whale. The Commander's long lance—six feet in
the iron, and four feet in the handle—is darted, at
arm's length, into the writhing carcass, up to the
very socket; and, before the fling of fins or tail can
reach, he has recovered a safe distance. The effect
of the wound in the vitals is speedily seen. The
previous white steamy vapour ejected from the lungs
has become tinged with red; and nature's powers,
as experience indicates, must soon decay. Convulsive action in the monster, as stimulated by this
inward stab, being at length suspended, the favourable moment is again improved. Another lance,—
darted in as quickly as the stroke of the tiger's paw,
—penetrates, for the second time, the vast viscera
of the whale; whilst the active agents of the attack
escape, as before, unscathed. The deadly thrust is
quickly repeated; and, as the capability of exerting
instant violence is diminished, the deeply stricken
lance is worked actively up and down whilst still
within, so that every movement effects an additional
wound, and the work of death is the more speedily
and mercifully promoted. Thick jets of blood now
issue from the blow-holes, and the sea, through the
wide space of disturbed waters, is tinged by the
overflowing streams; whilst boats, oars, and men,
are thickly sprinkled with the sanguinous dye.
Lanced, now, on both sides at once, with these formidable instruments of destruction, the dangerous ener-

gies of this vast animal become soon overpowered, and it now yields itself passively to its inevitable fate. One effort alone remains. The instinctive impulse or spasm of expiring vitality, — like the brilliant gleam or coruscation of the expiring taper, is expended in a series of tremendous death-throes. The writhing body of the giant captive is now thrown into strangely powerful action; fins and tail play with terrific violence, tossing up huge waves, and dashing the sea, for a considerable circle round, into foam. The prudent fishermen push off to a safe distance, and, looking on with the solemnised impression of a spectacle at once wonderful and sublime; leave the convulsions of expiring nature to expend themselves. The vital energies are exhausted; the huge carcass, so recently perilous in the energies of life, rolls, by the gravitating tendency of its formation, on one side, and slowly the helpless fin rises to the surface of the water, and inherent power of motion ceases for ever! Three hearty cheers from all hands engaged in the capture, with the waving and "striking" of the "jacks" displayed in the boats from which harpoons had been struck, announce to the ship the happy issue of the conflict; from whence, in turn, similar exulting cheers are heard loudly responding.*

* It will here be proper to notice, that in the foregoing description of this adventurous capture, we have taken occasion (in the way of illustration generally) to fill up the picture, in regard to some particulars of well known and prevalent experience, beyond the extent of the leading facts and outlines, or memorial records, specially before us.

We have remarked, in a foregoing chapter, on the economy in Providence, by which the fiercest quadrupeds, under human tact and intelligence, become subdued and tractable. Here, again, we are led to reflect on the economy manifest in respect to the *hugest* of the animal creation, whether on earth or in the ocean, whereby all become subject to man, either for advantageous employment, as to their living energies, or for purposes of utility as to the produce of their dead carcasses.

The capture of the whale by man, when their relative proportions, as to physical power and mass, are considered, is a result truly wonderful. An animal of a thousand times the bulk of man, with a corresponding superiority in strength, inhabiting an element in which man cannot exist, and diving to depths where no other creature can follow, with the capabilities, too, of abiding there for an hour together, is attacked by man on its own ground, not only in the tranquil Pacific, but in the boisterous northwestern seas; not only in the open seas of the tropics, but amid ice-bound regions around the pole; and in each region is constrained to yield its life to his attacks, and its carcass a tribute to his marvellous enterprise.

Why this result, with such disproportionate physical powers in conflict, should not only take place, but prevalently follow the attack, is satisfactorily explained on the simple principle of the Divine enactment. It was the appointment of the Creator that it should be so. And this, besides what we have already quoted from the sacred records of creation, we have again, by the inspired Psalmist and elsewhere, declared. Hence, as to the fact of the dominion of man over the inferior creation, Divinely yielded, we have the authority of this adoring appeal of God's inspired servant: —"What is man, that thou art mindful of him!" "Thou madest him to have dominion over the works of thy hands; thou hast put all things under his feet; all sheep and oxen, yea, and the beasts of the field; the fowl of the air, and the fish of the sea, and *whatsoever passeth through the paths of the sea.* O LORD, our Lord, how excellent is thy name in all the earth!"—Psalm viii. 6—8. No doubt this striking psalm has direct reference to the world's Great and Divine Redeemer; but what herein is true of the "Son of Man," is also, in respect to the consideration of the Almighty for man and his appointed dominion, true of men as a species. And so it follows, that the monsters of the deep, as well as the wild beasts of the earth, yield to this law of creation, that man should have the dominant power!

The whale, thus adventurously subdued, proved a large one of its kind, and a very valuable prize. Its special dimensions and produce, though not noted, may be very proximately gathered from the record (always made in the whaler's journals) which we have of the length of the largest of the laminæ of whalebone, viz. 11 feet 9 inches. According to the general

averages, as given in the "Account of the Arctic
Regions," (vol. i. pp. 449—478,) this specimen would
be about 56 feet in length, and must have yielded
about 20 tuns of oil, with about 22 cwt. of whalebone. The value of the capture (oil being *very low*
in price at the time) was about 500*l.*; but the same
capture, in the years 1801, 1813, or 1817, when
prices were *high*, would have been worth no less than
1000*l.* to 1100*l.*

Section VII.—*Remarkable Enterprise.—The nearest Approach to the North Pole.*

THE adventurous attempt to reach the *North Pole*,
like that of the " North-west Passage," may be considered as an enterprise peculiarly British. Of six
voyages expressly undertaken for this object, up to
the time, and inclusive of, Captain Buchan's, in
1818, there was no advance beyond the 81st parallel.
The highest latitude reached was by Captain Phipps,
in 1773, who advanced to 80° 48′. Captain Buchan's
farthest was about 80° 34′. And up to the present
day we have no account which can be fully relied
upon of any ship, discovery ship or whaler, having
approached within forty geographical miles of the
high northern latitude reached by my Father in the
year 1806.

The Honourable Daines Barrington, indeed, in his
discussion of the question of the " Probability of
Reaching the North Pole," adduces a great variety

of instances of the advance of whalers to far higher positions of northern latitude; but for the reasons stated in the "Account of the Arctic Regions," (vol. i. p. 42,) I consider the authorities from which Mr. Barrington derived his information as not satisfactory. As to the defectiveness in authority of *mere recollections*, or even of the notes of ordinary observers, in respect of adventures of this kind, I have a curious example in the "Account of a Voyage to Spitzbergen," by a Greenland Surgeon, who sailed in the Resolution professionally, on the very voyage on which my Father made his greatest advance northward. The author, in respect to this advance, thus states from his journal:—"May 28. Latitude by observation 81° 50'. Sea almost clear of ice, with a great swell; weather serene. Had our object been the making of discoveries, there was not *apparently* anything to have prevented us from going a good way farther to the north; at least we did not perceive any large fields of ice in that direction."

Now this is mainly erroneous. Instead of 81° 50', the highest latitude *observed* was only 81° 12' 42", and the statements as to the nature and position of the ice, are equally diverse from what those circumstances actually were.

My Father's notable enterprise in the attainment, probably, of the highest latitude that had ever been reached by man was made in the ship Resolution, in the voyage of 1806. Occupying, young as I was,

the responsible office of chief-mate in the ship, I have
the records of the adventure preserved in my journal
in all their essential or important details.

The entrance into the ordinary fishing-stations on
the western side of Spitzbergen was, on this occasion,
occupied by ice of extraordinary breadth and compactness. We entered it on the 28th of April, in the
latitude of 76° N., and, pressing northward at every
available opening, we reached the latitude of 77° on
the 7th of May. Several ships were then in sight.
On the 10th, a gale setting in from the S.E., we were
enabled to make considerable progress through the
encumbering ice, and soon left all our associate
whalers fairly out of sight; and from that time until
the 19th of June (after we had retraced much of our
progress southward) we never saw a sail.

Up to the 13th of May, indeed, there was nothing
unusual, as to the practice of my Father, in the nature
of the adventure. But on that day, being in latitude
about 78° 46', within sight of Charles Island, on the
western coast of Spitzbergen, he entered upon a new
and apparently dangerous enterprise,—the attempt to
find, whilst the sea was apparently *filled* with ice, in
this high latitude, a navigable sea still nearer the
Pole.

The ice around was singularly compact, and, to
ordinary apprehension, impenetrable. Northward of
us it consisted, as far as our view extended, of scattered masses of heavy drift-ice, closely cemented
into a compact body by recently formed *bay-ice*. To

attempt a passage herein, if such were possible, must, in any case, be a most difficult and laborious undertaking ; but if the compact body were entered, and not successfully penetrated and passed beyond, it might involve a risk, which a considerable fleet actually fell into, of the loss of the fishing season by a helpless besetment. There were indications, however, which my Father's experienced eye alone discerned,—of open water to the northward. The bright reflection of the snow-covered ices in the sky, constituting the phenomenon of the " ice blink," most certainly pointed out the continuous encumbering of the navigation for a considerable way in advance ; but, when elevated to the very top of the mast, he could perceive a bluish grey streak *below* the ice-blink, parallel to and skirting the horizon, which he deemed a sure indication of " clear water," *beyond* the proximate " pack." Yet this grey reflection, or " water-sky," might not be of any great extent? It might arise from a transient vein of water capable of being obliterated on the first change of wind? Were such the nature of the opening, it might prove, even if reached, the more dangerous trap, as its position was more advanced northward?

These considerations, of very serious import, were settled, happily, by another sign which the watchful navigator got sight of. He discerned, for short intervals, occasionally, a very slight motion, as he conceived, of the water in contact with some of the

large lumps of ice near the ship. His careful scrutiny
of the masses, under an anxiously watchful eye, at
length assured him that there *was* a movement.
Experience then certified that the movement could
only arise from a *swell*, and that the swell must proceed either from the main ocean, southward, or else
from some immense interglacial lake, or what is technically called "a sea of water," northward. That it
did not come from the southern ocean, the distance
to which he had penetrated, and the unmixed bright-
ness of the ice-blink in each of the southern quarters,
convinced him ; and that it *did* come from the northward he was able to satisfy himself, by carefully
observing the points or places on the masses of ice
where the alteration of level in the water was the
greatest; for this scrutiny sufficed to show, that the
axial position of the ice, which the motion pointed
out, was in strict parallelism with a wave coming
directly from the place of the "water-sky" to the
northward.

Encouraged by these indications, he determined
on leaving a position recently attained, where the
ship had some little room, and pushing, at all risks,
into the formidable body of consolidated ices still
beyond him. This arduous and adventurous purpose was commenced on the 13th of May, with a
moderate breeze (favourable to our advance) from
the south-west. Little progress was, indeed, then
made; but laborious perseverance, rendered effective
by a consummate application of all the means and

resources available for our furtherance, ultimately yielded the desired, and I might add, deserved success. During five successive days, a series of labours were carried on of the most energetic and persevering description. The transit through the intervening ice,—which consisted, as we have intimated, of extensive sheets of bay-ice, with heavy lumps and masses consolidated therein,—was urged by all the variety of aids that were known to be applicable. These aids, beyond the available force of occasional favourable winds, consisted in the cutting of tracks or channels with ice-saws, where the thickness was too great to be broken, or, where thinner, in breaking the ice under the bows by boats suspended beneath the bowsprit, whilst their crews rolled them violently, from side to side, as in "sallying;" in making canals, by well-laden boats being run across extensive planes of ice, where their weight, with that of their crews, might be sufficient to break the resisting surface; in "warping" through encumbered channels, or amid lumps of more ponderous ices; in "towing" with boats, or "tracking" by men on the ice, during calms, along any clear channels of water which might have been opened out a-head; and, finally, by *sallying the ship*, in aid of any of these resources, for widening the space in which she floated, so as to leave her free to move, where room might exist in advance. And here, I think it due to my Father to notice, in regard to the sallying of the ship,—an oscillating or rolling motion accomplished

by the running of the crew, simultaneously, from side
to side across the deck,—that the application of this
most important auxiliary process was original with
him, and, as far as I can remember, *now* for the first
time employed. It is a process, I may add, which
has subsequently been adopted by fishermen and dis-
coverers in general, as a mean which may often be
made effective when, *under all other means* for the
promotion of progress, the wedged-up or ice-bound
ship has become utterly immoveable.

The manner in which these various operations
were carried on was laborious in an extreme degree.
Whilst the crew were allowed but limited and distant periods for rest, my Father's exertions were
such as, except under the pressure of circumstances
involving the alternative of life or death, I think I
never saw equalled. Not only was he always at his
post directing, instructing, stimulating his men when
progress was being made or attempted, but often
looking out when the hands in general slept, or
continuing his superintending toils, watch after watch,
when portions of the crew had, alternately, their
intervals of rest. In that severe service, indeed, few
men could have so persevered. An extraordinary
vigour and strength of constitution enabled him to
accomplish, in labours of this kind, for which he had
so high capabilities, what most men would have
broken down in attempting.

His exertions and talents, as we have indeed anticipated, had their due recompense in the most suc-

cessful results of the enterprise. After passing an
icy barrier of extraordinary tenaceousness and compactness, as well as of formidable extent, we reached
a region, in the 80th parallel, of incomparably greater
openness than we could have anticipated,—" a sea of
water,"—to which we could see no bounds, but the
ice we had passed through on the south side, and the
land to the eastward.

Under a brisk gale of wind and with fine clear
weather, we were enabled rapidly to explore through
a considerable portion of its extent, the immense interglacial sea upon which we had entered. It was
found to stretch east and west, or E.N.E. and
W.S.W. more nearly, to an extraordinary extent,
and to be bounded to the northward as well as to
the southward by packed ice of undeterminable extent,—the two bodies of ice being ten to twenty
leagues apart. And within this vast opening, though
not till after the northern and southern ices had
closed together and joined to the westward, we made
the principal part of our fishery.

On the 28th of May, being in latitude 80° 8', we
killed our first whale; and within the next fortnight,
and near the same position, sixteen others yielded
their lives to our harpoons and lances. On the 29th
of June, only two-and-thirty days from the time of
our first capture, we completed our cargo, being "a
full ship," with the produce of twenty-four whales,
one narwal, two seals, two walruses, and two bears.
This cargo, by far the largest, I believe, of the

season, yielded 216 tuns of oil, and almost eleven tons of whalebone. The fishery, in consequence of the peculiar position of the ice, and the unusual inaccessibility of the best fishing stations, proved generally bad. Judging from the returns in my possession, comprising the successes of twenty-four of the Greenland whalers of that year, I should calculate the general average at about fifty tuns of oil per ship, or less than one-fourth of the Resolution's cargo. The united cargoes of nine ships, out of eighteen, from one port (taking, of course, the worst fished ships), exceeded only by a few tuns the single cargo which resulted from the singular enterprise of my Father.

But we return to the grand exploration of a region which, as far as conclusive records go, has not, before or since, ever been *navigated*.

In the first instance, after our arrival in this vast northern opening of the ice, we proceeded to the westward, and, finding no whales, tacked, when we had reached the longitude of about 8° W., in the parallel of 79° 30' N. We then stretched to the northward and eastward, proceeding, generally, near to or within sight of the northern "pack," for a distance of above 300 miles,—a direct uninterrupted progress in this high latitude quite unparalleled. On the 23d–24th, at midnight, an altitude of the sun, below the Pole, carefully taken with a fifteen-inch sextant by Ramsden, gave the latitude 81° 12' 42". We continued our progress until (early the following

morning) we had reached the longitude of 19° E.,
when our latitude, as estimated from the recent observation, was 81° 30′ N. This was our farthest advance northward, in which we had gained a position
within about 510 miles of the Pole ! Even then,
the navigation was still quite open to the E. N. E.,
(true) and from that point round to the S. E.; so
open, that, as we could certainly gather from the
appearance of the sky, we could have easily advanced
many many leagues farther in the direction we had
so extensively pursued.

Our situation, at our farthest advance, was singular
and solitary indeed. No ship, no human being, it
was believed, was within 300 or 350 miles of us.
Unquestionably, the crew of the Resolution now
occupied the most northern position of any individuals in the world ! The sea began to freeze and
threatened our detention. We had made no progress in the fishery, nor could we find any whales.
The seamen began to be anxious, fearful, and troublesome, so that abundant considerations urged our
return to the westward, where, as has been shown,
our commercial enterprise became so signally successful.

The accuracy of the determinations for the latitude
we have stated, was variously verified during our
progress both ways. Thus, going north-eastward,
we observed, May 23d, at noon, in lat. 80° 50′ 28″;
at next midnight, as we have noted, in 81° 12′ 42″.
At the succeeding noon, after above eight hours

sailing on our return, we again observed in 81° 1′ 53″;
and, still running south-westerly, we sighted at 8 P.M.
of the same day Hackluyt's Headland, some forty
miles still to the southward of our position.

We have spoken of this adventure as reaching to
the highest latitude ever attained, as far as we have
conclusive records, *by sailing*. Captain Parry, in
his Polar attempt of 1827, indeed, went beyond my
Father's greatest attainment a distance of seventy or
eighty miles; but this advance was wholly gained by
travelling across the ice. For with all the advantage
of a later period in the summer, and the penetration
of the loose ice by boats, the *travelling* had to be
commenced on attaining the latitude of 81° 13′.

In referring to this attempt, one can hardly refrain
from expressing regret at the success of an expedition so energetically pursued being marred by circumstances which, under better arrangements, might
have been avoided. For had the plan as originally
suggested, about twelve years before this adventure,
been acted on, I have no hesitation in affirming, that
a far greater advance northward, if not complete
success, must have attended the daring enterprise.
It falls not, indeed, within the object of the present
Memorials to take up again a question which is discussed in detail in a communication of mine to the
"Edinburgh Philosophical Journal," and published
in the number for July 1828; but it may suffice to
say, that the opinion offered just above has now the

sanction of the gallant conductor of the enterprise himself, who, in a letter published by the late Sir John Barrow, in his volume of "Arctic Voyages" (p. 313) states, that "he believes it to be an object of no very difficult attainment, if set about in a different manner." And, it may be added, a plan for that adventure is given in the letter now quoted, substantially embodying the characteristic points of my original scheme,* and, indeed, in no essential particular, except the suggestion for spending the previous winter at Spitzbergen, differing from it.

Under such support in the idea, from one of the best authorities amongst those experimentally acquainted with the difficulties of the undertaking, I am led, not only to an increased conviction of the practicability of the enterprise, but to the entertaining of the belief, that the triumph is yet in store for the daring and adventurous nation

> " Whose *flag* has braved a thousand years,
> The battle and the breeze ;"

when

> " The meteor flag of England"

shall wave upon the axial point of the world at the Northern Pole!

---

* This plan was first communicated to the Wernerian Society of Edinburgh, and published in the second volume of its Memoirs. It was subsequently set forth in a revised form, in the "Account of the Arctic Regions," published in the year 1819.

SECTION VIII.—*Devotional Habits, at Sea and
on Shore.*

AT this period of my Father's life, his religious
views and habits had become matter of personal
notice, and observation with myself,—so as, in certain
respects, to enable me to speak of them from distinct
recollections.

He always spoke of religion with reverence, and
manifested a particular regard for the institution of
the Sabbath.   He was strongly attached to the
Church, and attended its public services with most
reverential and undeviating regularity.   In theo-
logical views, he inclined to those of the Rev. John
Wesley, of whose character and principles he was a
great admirer.   Holding the system of that eminent
servant of Christ as auxiliary to the Church,—he
became much attached to it, so that, for a considerable
extent of his life, whilst by profession a churchman,
he was commonly the holder of a pew in the old
Wesleyan Chapel at Whitby, and, on the Sunday
evenings (after the services of the Church had closed)
was a constant attendant, not unfrequently being
accompanied by some members of his family, at the
religious services conducted there.

This feeling and habit brought him into personal
intimacy with the leading Wesleyans resident at
Whitby, and into friendly intercourse with the
officiating ministers of that body—to whom he always
evinced pleasure in showing kindness and hospitality.

It was in this connection that he made the acquaintance, and obtained the friendship, of the late talented Mr. Drew, to whose brief memoir, published in the "Imperial Magazine," which he edited, I have been indebted for several particulars in my Father's early life, not elsewhere to be found.

His attachment to the Wesleyans, indeed, had a further expression than that of often joining in their devotional services, and having much friendly intercourse with their members; for it extended to several instances of substantial good-will in the form of liberal contributions, as well as in loans of money in aid of their chapels.

My Father's distinctive regard for religion, and religious ordinances, was still further indicated by several circumstances which I had the opportunity of noticing as prevalent with him when at sea. Among these stand prominently in my recollection, the habit of having Divine service performed on the Lord's-day, whilst I accompanied him during his command of the Resolution of Whitby. On these occasions, the crew, summoned by the tolling of the ship's bell, were assembled in the cabin, where my Father conducted the service according to the form comprised in the Liturgy of the Church, and afterwards (for some voyages at least,) read portions, such as he deemed suitable, from some devotional book, or latterly, with my assistance as I advanced in years and experience, from a collection of plain, practical, and valuable sermons, which had been presented to me, for the purpose, by that amiable and eminent servant of Christ, the Rev. T. Dikes of Hull.

In addition to these devotional habits, may be noted, his habitual reliance on the guidance and protection of Divine Providence. This was variously indicated; not only by the use of pious expressions, which he was heard to utter when he was about adventuring on some perilous enterprise, or when he had been enabled safely to wend his adventurous way out of imminent dangers, but in respect to a habit, which he suggested to me, as fitting to be copied, of commencing his sea-journal with an appropriate prayer, supplicatory of the Divine guidance and protection, and of inserting at the conclusion of a successful fishery, a fitting collect of thanksgiving. The insertion of the latter, in a foregoing section, may claim the addition here of the form, as. modified out of a collect in the Liturgy, for the former, which I find uniformly inserted in many of my own journals: —" Assist us mercifully, O Lord, in this our intended voyage, and make it profitable to us, particularly by disposing us towards the attainment of Thy everlasting salvation; that, among all the changes and chances of this mortal life, we may ever be defended by Thy most gracious and ready help, through Jesus Christ our Lord, Amen."

The journal from which this form is quoted comprises, too, a poetic attempt by my Father,—an acrostic on my own name,—strikingly characterised by sentiments of devotion, humiliation, and adoration.

Another practice, which he prevalently pursued when at sea, in addition to the religious exercises already noted, was that of devotional reading when in bed. I refer to this particularly, not only because it was a practice that I had constant opportunities of observing, but because of the admirable contrivance (applicable, I think, to the condition of many invalids,) adopted for rendering this exercise and recreation convenient and agreeable without the labour of holding the book, or the prevalent exposure of the hands to the cold and often freezing temperature of his " state-room."

The contrivance consisted in an open deal frame, about eighteen inches by twelve inside, like a light flat picture-frame when empty, which, in my Father's case, was fixed by hinges to the bulkhead forming the inner side of his bed, so as to be turned up, flat against the side, when not in use. Being hung on an oblique plane, it became, when let down for reading, parallel to the position of the reader with his head, face upward, lying on a pillow. The distance from the face was adjusted to his own reading focus; but could easily be altered by different loops on the string or wire, by which the end opposite to that affixed by hinges was supported from the planking of the deck, or ceiling, overhead.

The book designed to be used was laid, with the open pages downward, upon the interior of the frame, where it was supported by three parallel wires, the side wires receiving the margins of the book, and the

centre wire the middle. These wires for the adjustment of distance were made to slide, by loops at their
ends, upon two other strong wires attached longitudi-
nally to the interior of the frame, so that the wires
could be readily adapted for a book of any size, from
a large quarto down to the smallest volume.

The condition of my Father's mind, in reference
to this all-important subject, I find particularly indicated in two of his letters, fortunately preserved,
which were written to me at the period embraced by
the present chapter, whilst, as a youth, I was attending the scientific lectures of the University of Edinburgh.* I select, with slight verbal correction, two
or three passages :—

"It is a great pleasure to us to learn that you
know the value of time which you have so nicely
divided to suit the lectures, etc.; but, at the same
time, beg leave to say, that we think you have made
a mistake when you say, 'I intend, if all's well, to go
to Mr. Wood's on Sunday, as, on that day, I have no
lectures to attend.' My dear son, I know it is too
much the custom to visit and take our pleasure on
the Sabbath-day, which ought to be strictly observed,
as the wise Author of all things has appointed. He

* From attendance on the instructive lectures and demonstrations
of several of the most eminent men of science and learning of the day,
during a considerable portion of two sessions, I feel it a matter of
grateful duty here, by the way, to say, that I obtained a larger measure
of general information and scientific knowledge than, within like period,
perhaps, any other existing instrumentality could have yielded.

has appointed one day in seven to Himself, that we
may rejoice therein and serve Him, as he has commanded us in the Holy Scriptures, desiring us therein
to search for wisdom, (as Solomon sought, and was
blessed with riches and honour,) which your Bible,
and *Sunday Lectures,* and your own prayers offered
up to God, will procure for you, and He will yield
His peace which passeth all understanding. We are
very poorly off indeed if there be no better things
in store for us than those of this world, which, compared to spiritual things, are all vanity and vexation
of spirit."

After a very gratifying notice of my "steady conduct," followed by some judicious paternal counsel
and warnings, the section of the letter now quoted
thus concludes:— " Hearken to the advice of a
Father, and walk in the *laws* of the *Lord*, which
you will find the greatest comfort this life can
afford."

The other letter, after a high commendation of
diligence in the acquisition of knowledge, and the
citing, for one's example, the names and enterprises
of many of the most distinguished scholars and
philosophers of antiquity, proceeds as follows:— " But
after a man may (like these distinguished examples)
have studied all arts and sciences, until he be as
great a proficient as Crichton, yet, *without religion,*
he will, at the latter end of his life, have, with Sir
John Mason, to exclaim,—*Seriousness is the greatest
wisdom, Temperance the best physician, and a Good*

I

Conscience the best estate. Therefore, my son, with all thy getting, get wisdom and understanding, and never be ashamed to carry a pocket Bible about with you, wherein you may find comfort in every state of life, and, at the same time, you will feel a thirst for every useful science, which, I flatter myself, you will not relax in pursuit of."

In conclusion of this sketch of my Father's views and habits, religiously considered, I may just notice, that, although his principles sometimes failed under special temptations, as in the case of Sabbath-day fishing, yet the feeling of reverence for the day appointed for rest and devotion, was seldom without some manifestation. If whales were pursued when incidentally seen on the sacred day, they were not sought for, nor were boats sent out on watch, as on other days, nor was ordinary work ordered or permitted to be done. During his latter voyages, however, his practice became more decided in this respect; for the fishery itself, pressing as, in a worldly view, its claims might seem, was suspended during the Sabbath; and the day was generally given to the appointed objects of the gracious and beneficent institution.

CHAPTER V.

FURTHER ENTERPRISES: GENERAL RESULTS.

SECTION I.— *The Greenock Whale-fishing Company.*

IN the summer of 1810, whilst I was on a recreative tour in Scotland, and visiting at the house of a merchant in Greenock, my adventures and experience in the northern whale-fishery became a frequent topic of conversation. This was the means of eliciting, in respect to several gentlemen with whom I had intercourse, a strong disposition to embark in this, to them, *new* department of commercial enterprise. My Father, at this very time, being on the point of retiring from the command of the Resolution, was informed of the circumstance, which speedily led to his forming a new and satisfactory connection with some of the first men, in character and position, in that enterprising port.

The associates, originally, were, I believe, George Robertson and William Forsyth (of the house of Messrs. Robertson, Forsyth, and Co.), and David Hyde, Esquires, who, with my Father, each holding equal, or one-fourth shares, constituted the new firm of " The Greenock Whale-fishing Company." Of this association, my Father was appointed the

managing partner, with authority to purchase and
fit out one or not exceeding two ships, for the
Greenland fishery, in which he was to have the
select or principal command.

Under this arrangement my Father proceeded to
London, and purchased two ships, only one of which,
however, the *John*, was ultimately appropriated to
this Arctic adventure.

The John was a Batavia-built *teak* ship, 316 tons
burden. To ships built of this species of timber,
almost indestructible in respect of ordinary decay,
my Father was very partial; and, in purchasing the
John, though she proved more expensive than was
expected (having cost 12,700*l.* to sea), he was not,
as to this peculiar and important quality of her
timber, disappointed. She proved a fine ship, an
admirable "sea-boat," and, except as to capacity,
which was rather too small, fully answered his
expectations.

No time was lost in entering upon this new and
responsible enterprise. The John sailed, on her
first voyage, in 1811, the season next succeeding my
Father's last command of the Resolution; and the
result, as to its successfulness, well satisfied the
sanguine hopes of the parties associated in the risk.
The cargo obtained was sixteen stout whales, which
yielded a produce of 200 tuns of oil.

With this commencement, the residue of the adventure of this concern amply corresponded. During
the four voyages to which the co-partnery extended,

103 whales were captured, and a produce of 837 tuns of oil, averaging 209 tuns a season, brought into port. In the last voyage of the series, that of 1814, thirty-four whales, yielding 249 tuns of oil, were taken; being, as to quantity, the best of all my Father's adventures. The cargo of the preceding year, however, was, on account of the very high price of oil, the most remunerative. The gross receipts of that year, on account of a cargo of 190 tuns of oil, and about ten tons of whalebone, amounted to the extraordinary sum of about 11,000*l*.!

The entire successes of this *fourth* command of my Father's, as thus exhibited, not merely equalled, it is seen, but actually exceeded any one of his former enterprises. Though his cargoes, however, were nearly double the general average of the fishery, there were now competitors, in this field of enterprise, who, *within this limited and particular period*, equalled or even outrun him in the race. The only accurate comparison which I am here enabled to make, is with respect to the successes of the Hull fishermen. And here I find two,—Captain Joseph Sadler, of the Gilder, and Captain Harrison, of the Walker,—whose enterprises during these four years were highly productive; having yielded, as to the former, something more than the John's cargoes, and as to the latter, just about the same amount. But in both these cases, it may be noticed, that the tonnage of the ships was advantageously larger than that of the John.

Before proceeding with an account of the concluding enterprises of the subject of these memorials,
we have an incident to notice, which, however
trifling in itself, may, it is hoped, interest the reader,
because of its characteristic nature and somewhat
amusing result.

Section II.—" *Cum au greim a gheibhthu.*"

THE capacity for receiving knowledge, and the
capability of applying the knowledge possessed, are
characteristics of very different qualities of mind.
The latter of these qualities is, *per se,* incomparably
the most important and valuable.   For one man, with
comparatively moderate attainments, but having a
facility in applying the knowledge he has acquired,
will be a far more useful member of society, and is
capable of becoming a more distinguished character,
than another of vastly superior acquirements in
learning, who does not possess the faculty of application.   Thus one, like the skilful mechanician, may
be able out of small variety of materials to construct
apparatus of indefinite extent of usefulness, or,
like the expert and talented smith, may be able to
construct out of one material every species of instrument (to use a sailor's phraseology), "from a needle
to an anchor," whilst another, though possessing
almost unlimited stores of materials, may have little
capacity for bringing them out and applying them
to purposes of usefulness.   The former case is that

of one who is of himself a practical artist in knowledge ; the latter, of one who requires others to bring
out and apply the knowledge which he has been
careful to store up.

My Father, in a truly eminent degree, possessed
the first of these characteristics of mind. Whatever
knowledge he might gain he was apt in applying,
and so applying, by the powers of a vigorous intelligence, as to make the result strikingly original.

The incident which I here record, was, indeed, of
itself, rather curious and amusing, than important or
specially useful. But in it we find developed an
order of mind which, if it possess but one fact of a
particular species, will, if occasion should ever require, or admit of its being done, turn that one fact
to account.

Whilst resident for considerable intervals of time in
Scotland, during his engagement with the Greenock
Whale-fishing Company, my Father had been thrown
into intercourse with some of the Gaelic speaking
population of the district. Some of their phrases
had struck him as being curious and forcible, especially in relation to the economics of worldly policy.
Among these, one phrase in particular had been
fixed in his memory—"Cum au greim a gheibhthu;"
which, being interpreted in Scottish idiom, he understood to imply, " Haud," or " Keep the grip you have
got."

The occasion on which this phrase, somewhat
felicitously, was brought into use, was the following:

—Returning from one of his voyages to the Greenland seas, whilst sailing from the port of Greenock, they had stretched, under a prevalence of southwesterly gales, to leeward of the northern shore of the island of Mull, forming part of the county of Argyle. The wind not availing for convenient progress on the destined course, they took shelter in Tobermory, near the head of the Sound of Mull. This port, as a site for commercial enterprise, was brought into consideration (undue consideration as the trial has proved) by the "Board of Trustees for the Encouragement of the Fisheries," a little more than half a century ago. The place naturally attracting my Father's attention, he went on shore with little delay. He proceeded to the inn first of all, and indicated his wish to the landlord to have dinner provided for him before he returned to his ship. The interval he naturally employed in examining the place and the neighbouring scenery.

During the time whilst he remained at the inn, and was in communication with its inmates, he observed,—when ordering his dinner, and when being waited on as he was eating, as also, subsequently, when he asked the cost of the entertainment he had received,—no language was spoken betwixt the landlord and his wife (who mutually contributed to his requirements) but the Gaelic. And on two or three occasions, especially on a discussion, as he fancied, of the important matter of the reckoning, there seemed to be a considerable difference of opinion betwixt the parties as *to the amount* to be charged. Nevertheless whilst by the significant action, and whispering tone, he gathered, or supposed he gathered, so much of the purport of the discussion, not one word of what was said, as they had justly inferred, could he strictly or certainly interpret.

But a trifling incident, by which his acquaintance with the maxim above spoken of was elicited, gave a new and somewhat astounding annunciation to his Gaelic-speaking hosts.

Some little time before his departure, being in want of some carbonate of soda, which he occasionally took for a not unfrequent annoyance of acidity at the stomach, a messenger, a little son of the landlord, was sent to the apothecary, to procure what was required, he being furnished with sixpence as payment for the same. On his return with the article it happened that the parents of the boy, who had just finished one of their Gaelic discussions, were both in the room, and were observant of his delivering the carbonate, and, along with it, twopence, the amount of the change. This, my Father declined receiving; but the boy, not thoroughly assured of the intention, turned to his parents for directions how to act, who, participating in his perplexity about retaining it, motioned him to return the pence again. On his second essay to do this, he was met by the most expressive and intelligible injunction,—" Cum au greim a gheibhthu,"—an injunction which the lad received with not less surprise than satisfaction.

Whilst my Father, with his characteristic self-

possession and coolness, practised this little device, he
was greatly amused in marking the wonderful effects
of his Gaelic maxim upon the minds and feelings
of his hosts. The mere utterance of a few words
in a language supposed to be unknown to their
guest, might have sufficed, under any circumstances,
to have occasioned some surprise; but the so felicitous an application of a national phrase in the
peculiar circumstances of the case, seemed absolutely to overwhelm them with consternation. For
they naturally inferred that their guest must be
familiar with a language which he had thus idio-
matically employed, and therefore that he must have
understood the discussions, designed to be *most
private*, which had been held in his hearing. From
that moment there was an obvious change of manner and conduct towards their guest by his hosts;
not that they were less respectful, but more cautiously
reserved; and it seemed not a little curious, after
so much of the native tongue had been heard, that
not another word of Gaelic was ever uttered by any
of the household in my Father's hearing so long as
he remained among them.

SECTION III.—*Subsequent and concluding
Enterprises.*

ON the retirement of my Father from the Greenock
Whale-fishing Company, the command of the John,
with the advantages and perquisites enjoyed by her

original commander, was transferred to his son-in-law, Captain Thomas Jackson. Having previously, during a period of three years, held a command in the transport service, besides having been associated with my Father in his voyages of 1813 and 1814, Mr. Jackson took up this somewhat novel service with that spirit, talent, and enterprise, which, in their action and results, were alike commendatory and successful.

My Father, meanwhile, whose spirit of enterprise, if not wearied, had become somewhat less constraining in furtherance of fresh undertakings, was content, for the first time during a period of above thirty years service, to remain for a season (that of the year 1815) unemployed. But, ill at ease in a condition of entire idleness, he undertook, for a couple of voyages, to sail out of Whitby (without engagement of property in the adventure) in charge of the *Mars*, a new ship of 343 tons, belonging to his old and steady friends, Messrs. Fishburn and Brodrick. The cargoes, in this instance obtained, did not correspond with those which had hitherto claimed for him an unrivalled superiority. They were still characterised, when compared with the results of the fishery in general, as superior; but superior only to an extent of one-fourth or one-fifth beyond the common average.

Another year of retirement from the sea-service, as a commander, succeeded his engagement in the command of the Mars; but the time was not spent, as before, without any professional object; my Father, in the autumn of 1817, having purchased, solely on his own account, another teak-built ship, the *Fame*, of 370 tons burden, originally brought into England as a prize from the French.

The fitting out of the Fame was deferred until a period very inconveniently late, under the idea, perhaps, of her being employed by the Government for Arctic researches,—just at this time proposed to be renewed ; and this idea he might well be supposed to entertain, because of the knowledge of the fact,— that it was in consequence of information communicated by myself to the President of the Royal Society, Sir Joseph Banks, that the attention of the Council of the Royal Society and the Government had been directed to the long dormant enterprise, and that that distinguished patron of science, with whom we both had frequent intercourse, was very desirous that I should be employed (having requested me to be sent for to London with this view) in the proposed adventure.*

Our expectations herein, however, I need hardly add, were altogether disappointed, and, so far as *expense*, at least, was concerned, much to the national disadvantage, as we could have accomplished one of those enterprises (the Polar research of 1818) at one-

---

* This fact having been differently reported and understood, the reader who feels any interest in the subject may satisfy himself, I believe, of the reality by reference to an article in the "Edinburgh Philosophical Journal," vol. xx. 1835-6, "On some Circumstances connected with the Original Suggestion of the Modern Arctic Expeditions."

tenth of the cost of the appointed expedition, and, at all events, with as much effectiveness; for, on that unfortunate occasion, *less* could not have been accomplished.

In consequence of the delay by this and other causes induced, it was not without very great efforts that the Fame was got ready for the fishery of the ensuing season, 1818. The requisite preparations however, were completed, whilst there was yet time for the adventure, and the ship, for the first attempt, being put under my command, sailed from Liverpool on the 2nd April. Having obtained, for the season, which was not a prosperous one, a good cargo, we returned, August the 18th, (as had been arranged) to Whitby.

In the following spring my Father re-assumed his habitual occupation in command of the Fame; but the great draught of water and somewhat sharp build of the ship, rendering the tide-harbour, to which, in this first instance, she had resorted, both inconvenient and unsafe, her port was again changed for Hull, to which, with but a moderate cargo, she returned. The next voyage, that of 1820, was, for the somewhat unfavourable season, a very successful one; that of 1821 was moderately good; that of 1822 returned only an average cargo; and the attempt of 1823 was prematurely arrested by the unfortunate destruction of the ship by fire.

The Fame had been fitted out for this contemplated voyage with unusual care and expense,—con-

siderable alterations and improvements, independent
of repairs, having been made; she had proceeded
northward as far as the Orkneys, where she had
taken up an anchorage for the completion of her
crew with boatmen, when the catastrophe, which
summarily frustrated the undertaking, brought my
Father's Arctic adventures at the same time to a
sudden termination; for after so long a pursuance
of his arduous enterprises, and the acquisition of a
handsome and ample competency, there were much
stronger motives for inducing him now to remain
on shore, "for the enjoyment of the fruits of his
labours," than to stimulate to further efforts in any
new undertaking.

The summary of these two latter enterprises, it
will naturally have been anticipated, does not correspond with that of the three-and-twenty years of all
but continuous successes. For though the cargoes
obtained in his six last voyages were, on the whole,
considerably above the ordinary average, yet they by
no means maintained the claim to superiority.

This change, however, in my Father's position as
a fisherman, admits of a satisfactory explanation. The
circumstances on which success was now dependent
had, in some most essential particulars, changed.
Superior knowledge of the Arctic ices, and consummate skill in penetrating and navigating the compact
or tortuous interruptions to the usual retreats of the
whales, which with *him* were so characteristic, were
now no longer available. So greatly had the whales

been reduced in number, apparently, by the enormous slaughter of their species during the last quarter of a century; and so much scattered had the residue been by the perpetual harass and attacks to which they had been subjected, that the positions, wherein the *opportunity* for making a successful voyage used to be constantly afforded, were now almost entirely deserted. Hence the enterprise and skill, enabling the fisherman to take the lead in penetrating the ice, which had been wont to be eminently rewarded, had now become of little avail. No one could calculate on the positions in which fish might be found. In places apparently most likely, not a fish, perhaps, was to be seen; whilst in circumstances least expected success might be met with. And although a few active, enterprising, and clever men, were now and then found taking a lead in respect to proportionate success, yet the fishery altogether had become very precarious; so increasingly precarious, indeed, that within about half-a-dozen years of this time the whale-fishery of the Greenland seas proved so utterly unremunerative, as to be all but abandoned as a distinct commercial enterprise. The port of Hull, for example, which during the whole period of my Father's command of a whaler had, on an average, sent out twenty-two ships annually to the Greenland fishery,—in 1828, only five years after he discontinued the pursuit, had only one Greenlandman, and the year following none.

His retirement from so active and enterprising a pursuit as had engaged the subject of these records during a period, altogether, of six-and-thirty years of his life, was by no means an event of unmixed benefit. It was far otherwise. For the effect of wear and tear on the constitution, whilst for this long period subjected to circumstances of peculiar anxiety and excitement of adventure, soon became apparent under the trial of absolute leisure and the deprivation of ordinary stimulus. It is, indeed, a well-ascertained characteristic of the human system, strikingly indicative of the wisdom and goodness of the Creator, to derive temporary energy from the very stimulus of the demands for energy. Thus strength, beyond all previous imagination, is often yielded for special occasions, whilst the capability of action is wonderfully maintained for the period of protracted necessity or duty. But the trial comes when the tension of the mysterious fabric of the human system has to be relaxed. The strength, for the occasion, being beyond the ordinary powers of renovation, is maintained by the nervous stimulant at the expense of a wear and tear which not only becomes apparent on the cessation of the undue exercise, but in aggravated proportion by reason of the natural reaction.

How far these operations in a too long continued stretch of the natural powers might have induced the inferior state of my Father's health, during the six years of his life succeeding the time of his retirement from the sea, it is impossible to say; though the fact of this deterioration of health, in the interval of leisure, was abundantly apparent.

SECTION IV.—*General Results of his entire Whale-fishing Adventures.*

IN conclusion of these records of my Father's Arctic enterprises, commercially, there remain yet to be given the *general* comparisons and results, in which we shall again find them to be great and pre-eminent. The materials for these comparisons, on my Father's part, are compendiously exhibited in the following summary of his various voyages:—

TABULAR VIEW OF THE SUCCESSES OF THE LATE W. SCORESBY, ESQ., IN HIS ADVENTURES IN THE GREENLAND WHALE-FISHERY.

No. of Voyage.	Year.	Ship commanded.	Cargo obtained.	
			Whales.	Tuns of Oil.
1	1791	Henrietta	clean.	nil.
2	1792	„	18	112
3	1793	„	6	90
4	1794	„	6	120
5	1795	„	25	143
6	1796	„	9	112
7	1797	„	16	152
8	1798	Dundee	36	198
9	1799	„	12	144
10	1800	„	3	45
11	1801	„	23	225
12	1802	„	20	200
13	1803	Resolution	13	164

TABULAR VIEW—*continued.*

No. of Voyage.	Year.	Ship commanded.	Cargo obtained.	
			Whales.	Tuns of Oil.
14	1804	Resolution	33	188
15	1805	„	30	196
16	1806	„	24	216
17	1807	„	13	213
18	1808	„	27	210
19	1809	„	26	216
20	1810	„	28	214
21	1811	John	16	200
22	1812	„	25	198
23	1813	„	28	190
24	1814	„	35	249
—	1815	[on shore.]	—	—
25	1816	Mars.	20	170
26	1817	„	6	82
—	1818	[on shore.]	—	—
27	1819	Fame	10	120
28	1820	„	10	184
29	1821	„	9	143
30	1822	„	6	70

The total number of voyages in which he held the command in the fishery, from first to last, was just thirty. The entire cargoes obtained, under this personal guidance, comprised the produce of 533 whales,— " a greater number," says his friend Mr. Drew, " than has fallen to the share of any other individual in Europe,"—with that of many thousands of seals, some hundreds of walruses, very many narwals, and probably not less than sixty bears. The quantity of oil yielded by this produce was 4664 tuns, of whalebone about 240 tons weight, besides the skins of the seals, bears, and walruses taken.

From hence we derive a general average, during the thirty voyages, of eighteen whales, yielding 155·5 tuns of oil per voyage; or, omitting the first voyage, which, for reasons stated in Chapter II., ought fairly to be excluded, the average would be 18·4 whales, yielding 160 tuns of oil for each voyage.

In comparison of the general average of the British whale-fishery, this, no doubt, stands singularly high. But not having the materials for the exact determination of this general comparison, we may take the Hull whale-fishery for our guidance, which, from the large number of ships regularly engaged therein, will, it is believed, afford a fair estimate. And this section of the fishery, we find, comprised, betwixt the years 1791 and 1822 inclusive, an average of twenty-two ships annually, the cargoes of which, during that period, averaged 84·5 tuns of oil a voyage per ship. Compared with this, it is seen, that my Father's yearly average was almost double the quantity!

It is not possible, because of the lack of accounts as to several of my Father's ships, to ascertain, except proximately, the actual value of the produce now determined; but, from the variety of information now before me, as to the marketable value of Greenland produce during a considerable majority of the years corresponding with these voyages, I have been enabled to calculate the gross proceeds of the whole thirty years adventures, in money, at 196,591l., or possibly a full 200,000l.!

The proportion of expenses due to these enterprises and results may, in like manner, be proximately
calculated. For, if the Hull fishery, with little more
than half of my Father's success, were fairly remunerative,—as it obviously must have been to induce
perseverance therein,—then, the residue of his catch
above that average may, mainly, be considered as
clear profit; for, in such estimate, we set off the
additional expenses incurred where there is superior
success against the actual remunerating profits in
the inferior success. On this estimate we should
have the value of, say, seventy-five tuns of oil and
four tons of whalebone for the clear profit; or, out of
a gross annual produce of the value of 6600*l.*, a residue
calculated to yield about 3000*l.* a voyage profit.*

This estimate would give the sum of 90,000*l.*, or,
omitting the first voyage, 87,000*l.* for the amount of
this individual skill and enterprise, divided, in the
shape of profits, among the owners embarked in the
general enterprise! On another ground of calcula-
tion, guided by the proportion of expenses in certain
known cases, the expenses were taken at two-fifths
the produce, which would reduce the profits (probably too low) to about 80,000*l.*

In setting forth this result as very remarkable, it is
with reference, it should be observed, to the instrumentality and *capital* employed. It is no uncommon

---

* This estimate of profits, though exceeding those of the Resolution,
already given, may be still maintained, on the ground of the price of
provisions and the high rates of seamen's wages and insurance, pertaining to a period, except as to one year, of continuous war.

thing for a sum like this, or much greater than this, to be realized in commercial enterprises; but, in such cases, there are generally many instruments and a large capital employed in the business. But here, under the one individual direction, there was but one ship employed, involving an investment of capital of from 6000*l.* to 12,700*l.*, or, on an average, not exceeding 9000*l.*, and this small investment yielding, through a series of about thirty years, no less a sum than 3000*l.* a year, being at the rate of 33⅓ per cent per annum on the capital employed.

SECTION V.—*Unusual Capture of Walruses.*

THIS incident, which belongs to the period of the Fame's voyages, is here introduced, in conclusion of the general series of my Father's Northern adventures, as presenting something of novelty in the modern whale-fishery.

The *walrus* or *sea-horse*, as the whalers designate it, is one of those extraordinary animals so prevalent in the Arctic regions, in which, like the whale, are comprised the mixed characteristics of the inhabitants of sea and land. The body, generally, from its extensive conformity, might be supposed to be that of a huge seal; but the head is peculiar, approaching the nearest, but only in rude and diminutive resemblance, to that of the elephant, as being somewhat square-faced, with a hard and massive skull, scarcely pervious to a musket-ball, and with two large external tusks pointing downward. The fore paws may be compared to webbed hands; the hind feet, in their ordinary position when at rest, form an expansive tail. The skin, covered with short hair, is of remarkable substance, so as to produce a strong, but rather porous leather, of about an inch in thickness. A thin layer of fat lies beneath the skin.

As met with on the coast of Spitzbergen, this animal is found of the length, ordinarily, of twelve to fifteen feet, and eight to ten feet in circumference. But specimens elsewhere found on the coasts of some Arctic countries, are represented as extending to twenty feet in length. The Spitzbergen animal, full grown, is about the bulk of an ox; its weight, as I have estimated it, being from fifteen to twenty-four hundredweight. But a twenty-feet walrus could hardly weigh less than three tons.

Though the tusks, the fat, and the skins, have a fair commercial value, the animal is never sought after as a special object of enterprise by the whalers, except incidentally, and very few are taken. Large captures, indeed, were occasionally made of sea-horses, in the early periods of adventure after the discovery of Spitzbergen; but these animals have seldom been met with by our modern whalers in any considerable number together, and their capture, consequently, has very rarely exceeded half-a-dozen in a voyage. No summary mode of killing them, indeed, had been prevalent or understood by which due advantage might be taken of any extraordinary opportunity. If met with in the water, where they might be attacked with muskets or lances, the chance of capture was but small, as the wounded animal would generally dive and escape. Formerly, I remember, harpoons of a *small* kind were provided expressly for the sea-horse; but with the whale harpoon, now only used, the tough skin of the creature is hard to be penetrated. If met with on shore or on ice, lances and muskets were more available, and in such positions the principal, though scanty, captures of modern times were wont to be made.

My Father's enterprise, therefore, in the case now referred to, was the more remarkable, not only because of the unusual number captured, but because of the novelty adopted in the mode of attack, by which mainly the success was gained.

Being on the coast of Spitzbergen, in the Fame, in the summer of 1819, when no incumbrance was met with from ice, my Father was induced to stretch into one of the fine picturesque inlets with which this remarkable region abounds, Magdalena Bay, where an extraordinary sight on the beach attracted his attention. Hundreds, if not thousands, of animals, which on their near approach proved to be sea-horses, were seen congregated on the sloping shore, thickly huddled together, basking in the bright sunshine and genial warmth of the sheltered position.

No one on board having ever seen anything of

the kind before, all were in a state of excitement, which soon became naturally diverted into ardour for conflict and capture. Measures were speedily concerted by which a due harvest might, if possible, be reaped out of this wonderfully stocked field. Muskets, evidently, could do little, as the vast herd, on being alarmed, would doubtless hurry into the sea, before the discharged arms could be reloaded, and harpoons could be of no avail. Lances and whale-knives, however, promised a better instrumentality, and especially one kind of the latter, the *tail-knife*, which in reality proved the most effective of all. This instrument, designed for making perforations in the tail and fins of the captured whale, when preparing to be towed to the ship, constitutes a portion of the furniture of every whale-boat, and consists of a nearly three-feet straight sharp-pointed blade, with a wooden handle of like measure. It resembles the blade of a cutlass, out of which weapon, indeed, this kind of knife is frequently constructed.

From accounts which at different times I have received from individuals participating in the affair, I am enabled to offer such description of the plan and proceedings as may serve, I hope, to give a tolerably correct notion of this curious and novel kind of exploit.

Well furnished with what appeared to be the best weapons for the attack, the boats set out on the adventure, spreading themselves, whilst at a distance, so as to make a simultaneous and warlike descent upon the beach.

As this animal is but imperfectly adapted for locomotion on land, and its progress, usually, sluggish and slow, there was a chance with the individuals which had adventured highest up the slope of doing some considerable execution among them. Though the walrus, ordinarily, appears singularly fearless,—it might be said, stupidly fearless,—yet the whole herd, in this case, was soon put into a state of commotion and alarm. The principal attack on the flanks having arrested several of the number, the general mass began a scrambling retreat, assuming a strangely formidable, yet otherwise grotesque appearance, whilst, in their haste, the huge carcasses were seen, in their mutual interferences, rolling one over another down the beach.

Two or three of the leaders of the attacking party,—the foremost among whom was, I believe, Mr. William Jackson, afterwards a successful commander, — perceiving the risk of the vast herd escaping before they should have time for any considerable success in captures, boldly threw themselves betwixt the affrighted walruses and the sea, so as, to the extent their means of destruction might enable them, to cut off their retreat. And now it was that the *tail-knife* was found to be a most admirable weapon for the occasion, its sharpness of point, and length of blade, yielding mortal results at almost every stroke, and its length of handle enabling its wielder to avoid the formidable tusks of the creature whilst attacking it close to hand.

K

The result exceeded the most sanguine expectations of the assailants. Many wounded ones, I believe, escaped into the sea, but a famous slaughter and advantageous spoil rewarded the adventure. One hundred and thirty of these animals remained as trophies of the sailors' victory, yielding, besides the corresponding quantity of hides, a large weight of tusks and teeth, adapted for dental purposes, and a quantity of oil, which, perhaps, we may roughly estimate at 1500 to 2000 gallons.

CHAPTER VI.

GENERAL CHARACTERISTICS AND MISCELLANEOUS NOTICES.

SECTION I.—*Superiority as an Arctic Navigator.*

MY Father's superiority as a fisherman, as exhibited in the foregoing pages, had an essential relation to his talents as a seaman and a navigator. The former, indeed, was in no inconsiderable degree a fruit of the latter; for it was his superiority as a navigator of ice-encumbered seas particularly, which, for a considerable series of years, enabled him generally to obtain a position in advance of his competitors, and thus yielded to him the best opportunities, whilst the ground was undisturbed, for making his fishery.

Not only, indeed, was he thus unrivalled among his associates in Arctic enterprise, but to him was due the introduction of a truly scientific system of arrangements, which, with their masterly application in practice, enabled him at all times, when " beating to windward " among crowded ices, or contending under the greatest obstructions and difficulties for a passage " to the northward," to take the lead.

The penetration of the Greenland ices, whilst in search of whales, being very prevalently pursued by

beating to windward, or by sailing "on a wind,"—
so prevalently, indeed, that, during a quarter of a
century from my Father's commencement in command, nine days out of ten, or more, were spent in
this description of navigation,—it became a matter
of grand importance to have the ship, as "to trim,"
"cut of the sails," ballasting, etc., specially prepared
for sailing "close-hauled."

For this style of navigation, the arrangements prevalent in the merchant service, at the time, were
most ill adapted. When without cargo, the ships
usually went in light "ballast-trim," and had their
sails cut so as to "bag" into a deep concave on the
side acted on by the wind, — conditions most unfavourable for "holding a good wind" or "working
close."

The whalers were thus universally circumstanced
at my Father's commencement. They went ordinarily ballasted, or, sometimes, "flying-light," not
only because of this being accordant with the general
practice with merchantmen, but with the view of
lessening the concussions against the ice when
coming into violent contact with it. My Father,
on the contrary, adopted a totally different system.
He caused such a large quantity of the lower and
second tiers of casks to be filled with water (to which
he subsequently added ballast of shingle or iron in the
interstices of the casks of the "ground tier"), that
the ship became as deep as with the third part of a
cargo; his sails he had made to stand as flat, under

the force of the wind, as possible; he had his ship
denuded of all useless spars aloft, as well as of sails
of little adaptation for sailing on a wind; and, finally,
the braces of the yards, and other running geer, he
had so adapted as to run free, and· as light as consistent with safety.

His ship thus presenting the least possible quantity
of surface to the leeward-tending action of the wind,
being so fully ballasted, and having her sails, so far
as he had the adjusting of them, adapted for standing
flat and "near the wind," he was enabled to make
a progress, in "windward sailing" among ice, which,
during a long period of years, defied all competition.

But the adaptation of the ship, it was apparent,
was not all. For the ships which he had himself
prepared for sailing on this effective system, retained
their advantage but very partially when they came
under other management. The Henrietta, which for
several years had taken the undisputed lead, was,
after my Father left her, beaten by the Dundee, and
the Dundee, in like manner, by the Resolution; and
not by the ship, only, which he now commanded,
was his former ship beaten, but by many competitors
besides. The loss of character in the ship he had
retired from, indeed, became a matter of much observation and remark both at sea and on shore; and the
circumstance was justly enough accounted for under
the quaint expression,—"she has lost her jockey."

It was, in fact, strictly so. The succeeding commander—clever as he might be in other respects, and

successful as one, especially, of my Father's training
was—had not the superiority in seamanship with
which the ship had formerly been managed. The
special adaptations, therefore, which my Father had
turned to such good account, were now only partially
available. Under considerable difficulties in the
navigation, or against hard competitors in the navigators, the once leading ship was liable to fail, and
very often did fail. The advantages provided in the
adaptation of the ship were, in such cases, lost in the
management. But where the navigator, as in my
Father's case, was pre-eminently skilful, the adaptations for windward and ice-encumbered sailing
became in the highest degree efficient, and resulted,
as has been shown, in an unrivalled superiority.

A commander may sometimes become distinguished
in war by successes acquired at an unusual sacrifice
of life. His resulting superiority may, in certain
cases, be dearly purchased. But there was no such
counteracting element in the pre-eminence, as an
Arctic navigator, gained by my Father. His deeply
ballasted ship might have struck heavier against the
ice than others, but she rarely was *allowed* to strike
heavily. Concussions not unfrequently fell to the lot
of other ships, light enough, and free to rebound as
they might be, by which, nevertheless, bows or sides
were stove in, and heavy expenses in damages consequently incurred; but no such disasters were encountered by him. His ship was wont to be a-head
in adventure, navigating the most difficult positions,

braving most alarming threatenings of the ices and the wind. But his ship went gallantly amid, and passed safely through, all these dangers. He knew precisely what his ship, in difficulties or dangers, *might* do; and that, under his commanding management, was done, and safely done. If, by the hundred chances which might thwart a difficult operation, — in the perpetual movements of the ice, the varying winds, the mistakes or defects of his helmsman, or the unpromptness of the men in management of the yards and sails,—his intended object or manœuvre should happen to be defeated, he was always ready, in his inexhaustible and well-considered resources, to save his ship from the imminent danger which a failure or blunder, in such cases, frequently involved. His quick apprehension of almost every possible contingency, served at once to develop and to bring into timely operation the resources which his fertile talent supplied; whilst his keen discernment of the quality and measure of the various movements of detached pieces or bodies of ice, as unequally acted upon by wind or currents, enabled him so to anticipate any probable risks, as to be prepared, however he might be baulked in his principal design, for some other furthering project, or, at all events, for a safe retreat.

The reality of my Father's superiority, as a navigator, now being described, admits, as to me it seems, of conclusive evidence in these two remarkable facts, —that, for the long series of voyages in which he held his first three or four commands, his ship, *in all difficulties where talent could be availing,* always took the lead; and that, for the whole time of his command, wherein he was wont to take the lead, equally in danger as in advanced position, he was always enabled, under the constantly recognised and sought-for bless-ing of Providence, to pursue his adventurous object safely, or without damage of any essential considera-tion, to his ship!

Within my own experience, whilst I accompanied him during nine voyages, from a mere child to adult age, I had perpetual opportunities of discerning his superiority over all the competitors we met with; and, during the same experience, I had repeated occasions for noticing with proud admiration, his wonderful skill in beating to windward amongst intricate ices, so as to leave every ship that we found near us in succession behind. In the morning, perhaps, at the commencement of a progress amid encumbering ices, I have seen around the Resolution, in various positions, to windward as well as to lee-ward, a considerable fleet of companion-whalers; and in the evening of the same day, after twelve or four-teen hours efforts in getting to windward, I have been able to see *no* ship whatever within the limits of vision from the level of the deck. On ascending then to the topmast head, where the extent of vision became vastly increased; I have generally found the pursuing fleet, bent on the same course, to be far away from us; some ships being left so much behind, perhaps, as to have disappeared, not from fog, or darkness, but from mere distance to leeward!

This striking feat of skill—differing in degree of course, according to the nature and extent of the navigable interstices of the ice, and the force and direction of the wind, with the sailing qualities of the competing ships likewise, as well as the seamanship of their commanders — was, as I have intimated, repeatedly performed under my own observation. But the like triumph of superiority was also gained, and that on different occasions within my personal observation, when the competing progress was being made through a compact body of ice into the northern fishing stations, and where the penetration, in anticipation of the general fleet, gained its due reward in an early and superior success.

The voyage of 1806, described in Chapter IV. Section VII., exhibited a striking example of the successful application of this talent; and in that of 1809, the same result was interestingly realized.

We had taken the ice, in the latter case, with the view of penetrating the barrier betwixt the free northern ocean and the fishing stations in the seventy-ninth and eightieth degree of latitude, along with a large fleet of other whalers. For some days, whilst no material progress could be made, we remained in varying relative positions presenting but little decided advantage. At length, when circumstances gave room for the due exercise of talent and perseverance, we made a progress so much beyond that of our associates, that we gradually left them, farther and farther, behind us, until the whole of the fleet were out of sight. We thus gained the "northern water" considerably before the others, and, falling in with whales in abundance, soon commenced a most encouraging fishery. By and by, others of the fleet began to make their appearance; and I well remember the astonishment of the captains and men of three ships which came close up to us on the 5th of June, just as we had taken in our *fourteenth* whale, whilst they had only obtained six amongst them. One of these ships had been near us, or in company with us, on the 27th of May, the day on which we succeeded in surmounting the icy-barrier. She, however, had only made the same passage the day before this, and had made but trifling progress in the fishery.

As there is no portion of the navigable ocean throughout the globe, at all comparable, as a field for the exercise of superior talent in seamanship, with the ice-encumbered regions around the poles; so my Father's capabilities in this beautiful practical science, had, at once, the requisite scope for their abundant exercises, and their admirable triumphs. No matter what the species of manœuvre or operation might be, he was equally superior in all. In "making fast" to the ice in gales of wind—an operation of singular difficulty and ofttimes of no small risk,—the manner in which he brought up his ship to the nearest possible proximity with the place of the ice-anchor, afforded time and opportunity for getting out and attaching the mooring hawser, and then, with progressively reduced sails, eased the ship's action on the rope till

fairly brought up, head to wind,—was in the highest
degree masterly and beautiful. Repetitions of trial,
and failure on failure, with much useless toil and
re-setting of sails, and, not unfrequently, with very
hard blows against the ice, were matters of such
perpetual experience among the inferior navigators
engaged in the service, as to render the operations
we have just attempted to illustrate, the more conspicuously admirable.

SECTION II.—*Natural Science.*

To my Father's *natural science,* or original, almost intuitive, perception and application of scientific
principles, I have already made repeated allusion.
But this characteristic of originality, as well as superiority of mind, deserves, I think, more special consideration.

Having to deal with circumstances perpetually
varying, and frequently presenting features entirely
new, the profession to which he had devoted himself
afforded almost the best possible opportunities for
the development and application of this quality of
mind. And, in a greater or less degree, every
voyage he undertook as commander served to elicit
this admirable characteristic. Those who understood
him not, very naturally ascribed many of his novel
proceedings to eccentricity, and these might be liable
to run into this very usual extreme; but, for the
most part, the apparent eccentricity was, in reality, a

sound result of reflective, philosophical consideration. I might adduce some incidents, perhaps, in which the originality of conception was pushed into an extreme: yet I could recal, possibly, hundreds of others in which such conceptions resulted in proceedings at once admirable, in their fitness, and, as such, worthy of imitation.

1. Take, for example, the process of *sallying* the ice-bound ship for relieving her of any remediable pressure, and giving free action to the power of wind or "warps" for promoting her progress. And in this we have an adaptation of a previously unapprehended mean and provision, always at hand, possessing extraordinary capabilities as a mechanical force. It may not be uninteresting to elucidate this fact.

Suppose a ship, navigating the Arctic seas, to be held firmly on the sides by the contact of two large sheets, or numerous compacted pieces, of ice. The ice just a-head may be less compact, or there may be a proximate channel, available for "boring" or sailing, if the existing pressure could be relieved so that the ship might be free to move. For the relief of this *lateral* pressure, no mechanical force, except the action of the wind on the sails when coming somewhat in the direction of "the beam," had heretofore been considered as available, or had been applied. But my Father's device afforded a novel, as well as a powerfully available, agency. In what degree powerful is easily estimated. The ship, in the case referred to, we will suppose is tolerably flat-sided (like the Resolution), and floats, ordinarily, at the depth of the greatest width. Now the power yielded by sallying may be considered as corresponding with that obtained by a wedge acted on by a heavy weight; the *wedge*, in this case, being the portion of the ship's side that becomes depressed, operating by virtue of the expansion of the ship's *width* when heeling, and the *force* acting on the wedge being the weight transferred from an even distribution with an upright position of the ship, to an accumulation of weight on one side, inducing a heeling position. Let the extent of heeling be considered as a " streak" of nine inches, in which case, as the opposite side will be proportionally and equally raised, the width of the line of flotation will be increased, altogether (in a main breadth of 26 feet), about half an inch, or a quarter inch on either side. The depressed side, then, in its progress under water, as far as nine inches, will have expanded a quarter of an inch in width, and the raised side an equal quantity; and both sides will act on the contiguous ices with the mechanical force of a wedge of nine inches long and a quarter-inch at the thick end,— exhibiting, on the ordinary mode of calculating the power of the wedge, a gain of power for either side in the proportion of twice the length of the wedge,* or 18 inches, to a quarter inch, or as 72 to 1.

* The inexperienced mechanic is liable to be puzzled with the action of the *wedge*, because of its being estimated, in some modes of its appli-

The force acting on these wedges is that of the *weight* of the men employed in sallying, when all are placed on one side of the deck right over the head or back of one of the wedges. In a whaler carrying fifty men, the weight available for this purpose, say that of forty-six or forty-eight of the crew, may be estimated at about three tons, one half of which only would act downward, the other half being expended in the resistance upward, of the opposite side.

Hence the mechanical force hereby derived, as represented by these data, would appear to be that of two wedges of a power of seventy-two to one, each acted on by a weight of a ton and a half, that is, a

cation, in the *double* proportion of its length to that of once its thickness, giving to it, *apparently*, twice the force of the other mechanical powers. It may not be unfitting, for the sake of our young readers, to explain the little difficulty. The wedge when acting against one fixed and immoveable body for the removal of another body, has then, only, the like force as the lever,—a force proportionate to the extent of space passed over, in driving, by the length, with respect to the increase in the thickness, of the wedge; but when acting for the separation of two bodies, both moveable, both sides then become effective, and it necessarily exerts double that power. And so does the lever. For if the lever be employed in like manner, the action in separating two moveable bodies will be just double that of its ordinary action where the fulcrum is absolutely fixed. This, indeed, is obviously the same with all the mechanical powers. Action and reaction being equal, the power exerted in raising or moving one heavy body must be exerted reversely against the earth, or other fixed body serving as a fulcrum to the lever, or for the attachment of one extremity of a tackle or series of pullies, or for the securing of the capstan spindle. Let the attachments of the machine and its object, however, be both afloat, and then any of the mechanical powers, like that of the wedge, will have an efficiency of double that of its ordinary operation where one part is a fixture.

force of the weight of 108 tons acting towards the separation of the ice and ship on each side. But only half the amount of these two forces, it will be obvious, comes effectively into operation; for the wedges, being on *opposite* sides of the ship, act antagonistically, thus spending one-half of their power against each other, in the compressing of the opposite sides of the ship together. The force really in operation, then, serving to push off the ice from each side, or tending to separate the compressing masses of ice, will be equivalent to two weights of fifty-four or altogether to a weight of 108 tons.

If there were no resistance either from the *friction* of the ice on the ship's sides, or from the *stability* of the ship, the estimated mechanical force, for the case assumed, would no doubt take effect. The resistance from friction cannot, it is evident, be determined; but that of the ship's stability might be easily represented. At the *commencement* of the heeling position, however, the resistance from this source would be but trifling. In its actual influence, in ordinary cases, the stability might abstract, perhaps, a quarter or a third part from the entire force exerted, but still leaving a free action equivalent to the weight of seventy or eighty tons towards the separation of the ices, right and left.

But the force ultimately brought into operation, after a sallying motion is once obtained, becomes still greater and more effective,—acting now and then, in the nature of concussion from the momentum of a

portion of the ship's weight, as thus may be illustrated:—

The weight of the crew, in the outset of the operation, being placed all on one side of the deck, and
then suddenly transferred to the other, will, after the
overcoming of the friction originally induced by the
ice, cause the ship to heel, and, on the reversing of
the action (by the men running back again across the
deck) the direction of the heeling will be also reversed.
The process being carried on with a strict attention
to the adjustment of the moment of the running of
the men (indicated by the word of command, "over")
to the time of change in the natural oscillations of
the ship,—these oscillations (supposing the ice to
be gradually receding) will increase to a maximum,
whilst the incidental concussions of the ship's sides
against the contiguous ices will act as a "ram" on
the wedge-like expansion of the width of her two
broadsides. The additional force thus incidentally
applied, it is evident, may be enormous. Hence the
wonderful effects sometimes produced by my Father's
ingenious device of sallying,—effects not less important and striking when "clawing" to windward
of masses of ice in boring, when, by the mere action
of the wind on the sails the ship may have come to a
stand, as when stuck fast betwixt equally compressing
ices on both broadsides at once. The moment the
sallying is perceived, the ship realises such relief
from both pressure and friction, as to start a-head as
if acted on by a magical power!

It hardly requires, perhaps, to be explained, that our investigations of the operation of sallying in urging a path through encumbering ices, are, strictly, only illustrative. For the action of the ship's side which we have considered as that of a regular straight wedge is, in reality, curvilinear, and, ordinarily, would be unusually thin at the apex, thus giving, at the commencement of the heeling movement, a much higher degree of mechanical power. The *extent* of the compression on the ship's sides, too, we could only consider in a particular case, such as one of thin ice, or ice touching the sides to no great depth. In case of compression from thick ice, having contact with the ship's sides to a considerable depth, the resistance to the sallying would, of course, be much increased, and, by consequence, the operation less effective.

It may just be added that the principle of sallying is evidently capable of still more powerful application by aiding the *weight* of the men, in the first instance of movement, by auxiliary loads of guns, chains, casks, or other heavy bodies transferred to one side of the deck; or, in a still higher degree, by an auxiliary mechanical force derived from a "purchase" from the ship's lowermast, or topmast head, to an anchor fixed in a distant part of the ice on either side. An enormous power, it is evident, might be derived from a leverage of this kind, sufficient almost to compress or squeeze in the very timbers of the hull.

2. Another example of the application of the principles of natural science, may be adduced with respect
to my Father's practice in the capture of certain harpooned whales. In the most usual habits of the
mysticetus, when struck in the Greenland seas, it
descends to a considerable depth, generally 600 or
700 fathoms, and, after an interval of about half an
hour, or so, returns spontaneously to the surface for
respiration. But sometimes, especially when a taught
strain has been held on the line, the whale continues
to press so determinately into the depths of the ocean
that it dies by a process similar to drowning. In
that case the heaving up of the capture becomes a
matter of great labour and difficulty, and, because of
the liability of the harpoon to draw, or of the lines
to part, of much uncertainty as to the result. It is a
matter, therefore, of much importance to avoid the
possible contingency of a harpooned whale "dying
down." The process ordinarily adopted for inducing
the return of the fish to the surface, after the downward course is suspended, is to haul on the lines
as soon as any impression can be produced, so as to
stimulate to action and urge an ascending motion.
In very many cases this process is effective, but by
no means in all. For sometimes so desperate and
continuous is the effort to get down that, when necessity might urge a return to the surface for respiration, the power to return no longer remains, and the
helpless monster dies at its utmost depression.

My Father, with his peculiar felicity of consideration and device, assumed a measure of proceeding as *apparently* unfitting as it was novel in its character. When the usual processes for the obtaining of the fish's return to the surface had failed, and no prospect remained but that it must die where it was, he would throw off the turns of his line round the stem or "loggerhead" of the boat, and allow an extent of fifty or a hundred fathoms more to run freely out and sink in the water.

The meaning of the device was this:—The entangled whale had no doubt descended deep in the water, as its ordinary mode of escaping from its natural enemies; but the attachment and restraint of the line it could not escape from. It was an instinct with it, therefore, as he conceived,—as in the case of some well-known quadrupeds, which may be driven but will not be led,—to resist the restraining force, and to struggle to distance the point from which the restraint proceeds. The untoward effect of this instinct, my Father supposed, might be diverted by rapidly slacking out a large extent of the entangling line, so that it might sink *below* the place of the fish, and so *draw downward;* for the same instinct which had incited it so perseveringly to dive, might naturally be expected to urge it, under this change of circumstances, to an upward course.

The experiment on being tried proved, in different cases, successful. The whale, stimulated to a new course by a new direction being given to the restraining line, returned to the surface, where it was received by its waiting assailants, and, when deprived of its life, became a prompt and easy prize, instead of an uncertain, hard-earned object of pursuit!

3. Besides the cases just recited of aptness in natural science, another occasion is before my recollection in which, during his varied adventures in the whale-fishery, this characteristic of mind, with my Father, was strikingly developed. A large whale had been "struck" on the borders of a vast sheet of ice, denominated a "field," which took refuge beneath the frozen surface, and, after suffering the deprivation of air for a period too considerable for its capabilities of endurance, died there.

After a long interval of patient waiting, on the part of the whalers, for the turning out of the expected capture (for the compactness of a firm field of ice generally obliges the whale to return to the outside for the purpose of respiration), they proceeded to haul on the line to try to facilitate their expectation. But when as much force had been applied as the line might safely bear, their efforts came to a stand. There was no reactive motion indicative of life in the whale, nor any progress towards its withdrawal, if dead.

Various repetitions of a similar effort, after slacking out a quantity of line to give some change to the direction of the tension, ended in the same discouraging manner; so that a doubt arose whether the harpoon were yet attached to the line, or

whether it might have got entangled on some submerged irregularity of the ice.

My Father at length left the ship to give his personal attention to this difficult business. His first
care was to examine the line at its fullest tension;
but the exact direction was not discoverable because
of the thickness of the verge of the ice. Slacking
out, therefore, a considerable quantity of the line, he
caused the boat to be backed off to a little distance,
and, whilst it was kept off as much as possible by the
oars of several boats attached, the line was hauled in,
till, becoming nearly horizontal by tension, its direction beneath the ice could be clearly determined.
By this direction he traced, by the eye, an imaginary
corresponding line on the surface of the ice-field,
which, by means of numerous irregularities and
hummocks, he was enabled to do satisfactorily,—
noticing particularly a very high and conspicuous
hummock in this exact direction, and at about the
distance to which the quantity of line run out might
be supposed to reach. His next step, and that a
truly scientific one, was to try to vary the line of
direction, so that he might determine, by the intersection of lines, the position of the harpoon. This
he effected by again slacking out the line, but to a
much greater extent, and then causing the position
of the boat to be changed by rowing slowly in a
direction parallel to, and at some distance from, the
edge of the ice, until the new direction might make
a large angle with that previously determined. Time

being allowed for the rope to subside into its position of rest, tension was given to it, as before, and another imaginary line traced by the eye on the ice. My Father now perceived that the point of intersection corresponded very nearly with the position of the remarkable hummock, almost a mile distant, before noticed, and that it must be immediately beyond it.

Taking a whale-lance in his hand he walked over the ice to the place, and *just beyond* the hummock he found a thin flat surface of much younger ice. Striking his lance repeatedly into this, he gradually effected its perforation; when, to his no small delight and to the amazement of the men who had followed his steps, his lance struck against a soft and elastic substance beneath: — it was the back of the dead whale!

Aid of hands and instruments being now obtained, the thin sheet of ice was partly cut out and the fragments removed till the attached line could be got at. When effected, it was again slacked out of the boat, and the end firmly secured to the slender part of the body of the fish adjoining the tail. The two lobes of the tail were then partly cut off, so as to hang down in the water as sustained by a slight attachment, and thus by their gravity to help to sink the carcass whilst they no longer were calculated to catch the irregularities of the submerged surface of the ice, as the tail, when perfect in structure and position, had previously done. A considerable weight, I believe, in sand-bags, was also hung upon the "bight" of the line for helping to sink the fish clear of obstructions above, and, finally, the line being hauled on in the boat from whence the fish had been originally harpooned, it progressively yielded to the force applied, and in due time the loud and cheerful huzzas of the sailors announced the completion of the capture in its appearance outside!

SECTION III.—*Improvements and Inventions.*

WE have had occasion, in the course of our memorial records, to describe several important inventions or improvements of my Father's in connection with his professional occupations. There remain yet to be mentioned a variety of other contributions, of a like order, to Greenland apparatus or operations pertaining to the fishery, and also to objects of public consideration generally.

As to whale-fishing apparatus and operations, his contributions in the form of new contrivances and improvements were numerous, and, many of them, of considerable importance.   These, we shall not attempt to describe in any measure of detail, but chiefly in the manner of notices

In the stowage of his ship, for the economising of space and facilitating the depositing of cargo, his improvements were valuable.

His *casks* he had built on a plan adapted for the accurate filling of the space in the " hold," comprising special deviations from the general size and form in the introduction of large "leagers" for the midships (on the kelson), adjusted, in length, to the exact spaces of the stantions of the hold beams, as also of narrow, short, or irregularly formed casks for the extremities of the hold, fore and aft.

The *deck* on the hold beams, instead of being laid, as usual, in a continuous series of planks, was cut up into hatches, and laid level betwixt the beams, so as, whilst forming a flat and even platform when laid down, to open out the hold, on the removal of the hatch - like planking, without other incumbrance against the stowing and filling of the casks beneath, except the naked beams and their essential fastenings.

In the suspension of the *boats*, with regard to facility in lowering or hoisting, as well as for safety, his improvements were of great importance.

It had been the practice in whale ships' equipments, to suspend the boats, usually seven in number, in double tiers at both *quarters*, one at the "waist," on each side, and one over the stern. The arrangements for these objects were at once clumsy and incommodious. In place of the huge lofty beams across the quarter - deck, from the extremities of which were suspended the four "quarter boats," my Father substituted compact, but lofty oak "davits," which, with their associate "skids" (upright timbers against which the sides of the boats press and slide), were removable when not required. For the double tier at the quarters, he substituted an additional length of boats over the main chains, thus constituting an even running series of three lengths of boats, having the advantage of great facility in being lowered or hoisted, as well as a much improved security against accidents in the passing of hummocks of ice, or from the sea in gales of wind, to which the *lower* quarter-boats, on the old plan of suspension, were frequently exposed.

In *fishing* and other *apparatus*, my Father made various improvements. In the harpoon, the improvement consisted mainly in the mode of keeping it in condition for use,—*bright* and *clean* as well as sharp; but in the lance he altered the form of the blade, which had usually been sharp - pointed and only moderately hardened, for a somewhat rounded point and a better quality of steel with greater hardness,— the advantage of which was, that if striking against a bone, the point was not liable to be fixed by its deep penetration, nor to be turned up or broken, as often happened, by the collision.

Some of the " flensing " apparatus, and one or two of the instruments used in " making-off " the blubber, he variously modified and improved, substituting for some very clumsy contrivances employed in the latter operation, compact and well-adapted instruments.

The *ice-drill*, a handy and very effective instrument for setting an *ice-anchor*, was his contrivance, being a great improvement upon the old *ice-axe*.

The talent for contrivance and improvement, as thus practically evinced, was by no means limited in

L

its exercises to subjects of a mere professional nature. The town and harbour of Whitby, with regard to some important modern improvements, have reaped conspicuous benefits from my Father's suggestions.

His views on various matters of improvement in the town and harbour, with their respective approaches, were first put forward in a pamphlet which he published in the winter of 1816-17; and in 1826, about three years after his retirement from the sea, the substance of the original pamphlet, revised, extended, and illustrated by engraved plans, was again brought out under the title of "An Essay on the Improvement of the Town and Harbour of Whitby, with its Streets and neighbouring Highways; designed also for the Maintenance of the labouring Classes who are out of Employment."

The improvements herein suggested, appear so far to have commended themselves to the local executive authorities, that, in certain important particulars, corresponding improvements have already been carried into effect.

Of these various suggestions, the one by far the most important of all is evidently that designed for deepening the harbour-channel, and rendering the entrance more safe and accessible.

For a long period the harbour of Whitby had been protected, seaward, by two principal piers,—one running from the eastern cliff about 215 yards, in a north-westerly direction, and the other (a fine specimen of massive and substantial architecture) running north-

north-easterly, along the western side of the harbour, and extending beyond the line of the west cliff, a distance of about 940 feet into the sea. This longer pier, at the time my Father wrote, stretched out a distance of about 100 yards (reckoned from the general direction of the coast) farther than the head of the other, leaving, however, a clear width, for the entrance of the harbour, of about ninety-two yards.

The effect of this arrangement, as to the extension of the western pier so far beyond the other, was, as my Father well observed, extremely injurious; for a deep bed of sand was constantly found encumbering the entrance by the formation of a " bar," which not only rendered the channel tortuous and incommodious, but not unfrequently diminished the otherwise available depth on the firmer bed of the river to an extent of several feet. And besides this mischief to a harbour almost drying at low water,—the access, with *scant* winds from the westward, was rendered at once difficult and dangerous because of the flood-tide sweeping strongly across the harbour-mouth to the eastward, and tending, by its leeward set, to carry the ship attempting to enter, against, or beyond, the left-hand pier, and thus to risk her total destruction by stranding on the contiguous dangerous scar.

For the correction of the evil and danger thus, apparently, induced, my Father proposed the extension of the east-pier by a bend in a more northerly direction, so that, whilst the reflux of the harbour water, and the natural stream of the *Esk*, might,

within the narrowed and extended channel, carry
out the loose sand of the bar into the sea, and thus
deepen the entrance,—the projection of the east pier
might serve at once to guide the tidal coast-stream of
flood with more force into the harbour, and to render
the access more easy and safe by such a protection
immediately under the lee of any ship coming in
with a scant wind from the westward.

This plan, with some little deviation, has already
been carried into effect. The pier has been length-
ened in a N. by W. (westerly) direction, by sections
of fifty feet at a time, in the proposed direction; at
each section, now increased altogether to about 300
feet, the channel has been found to be deepened and
rendered less tortuous, and the entrance has become
more safe,—exactly as the projector of the improvement had anticipated.*

A grand improvement, as to the change of aspect
and accommodation, to the inner harbour, was also
suggested by my Father, but has not yet been carried
into effect. The improvement suggested was for the

---

* This important work not being yet brought to a completion,—the
ultimate and abiding influence of the alterations cannot be accurately
predicted. The entrance of the harbour, by the new extension of the
east pier, having been narrowed, perhaps too considerably, a temptation
is offered to cast the terminal length, or head, in a bell-mouthed fashion
more easterly. If such an arrangement were made (as my intelligent
connection, Mr. Jackson of Whitby, suggests) it *might* produce a very
mischievous effect by giving a broad fan-tail exit to the escaping ebb-
tide waters, and so diminishing their force at the very point where con-
centration and compactness of efflux are of the greatest importance in
scouring the entrance and keeping it clear of sandy deposits.

formation of the large space, above bridge, which is filled at spring tides from the sea, into a permanent floating-dock,—a scheme which he conceived could be easily effected by a wall, with gates, across the harbour, at, or near, the place of the present bridge.

The effect of such an arrangement, indeed, is not easy to be anticipated. How far the overflow of water would suffice to keep the channel clear of sandy deposits? or to what extent the body of debris and shale from the mines above might, in such case, make lodgment in the bed of the inner harbour? cannot be certainly determined. Yet as there are existing wears at some distance from the town across the river bed, and no permanent deposits, except in their immediate contiguity, I believe, induced, it seems not improbable but that with a sufficient number of escape sluices in the seaward bounding-wall, the efflux, whilst carrying off the considerable supply of water yielded by the river, might suffice, at the same time, to urge outward the descending debris, and keep the channel free.

In conclusion of these notices respecting my Father's inventions and suggestions for improvements, it will not be out of place to add the substance of an interesting and curious autograph document (which fell into my hands after his decease) referring to other speculations, contemplated evidently as practicable, though neither explained, as to principle or process, nor attempted to be carried out.

The document, which as to its manner reminds one of the Marquis of Worcester's "Century of Inventions," bears the date of London, 23d December, 1824, and is aptly entitled—"Hints; or Outlines of Improvements conceived by W. Scoresby." These outlines, of which the following are pretty nearly literal and verbal extracts, are, in the original, thus introduced:—

"How swift is a glimpse of the mind!
　　Compared with the speed of *its* flight,
　The tempest itself lags behind,
　　And the swift-winged arrows of light!"

"During forty years occupation at sea, (the document then proceeds to set forth,) when duty called me to watch, my mind was, at intervals, employed about many things which might have been made useful to the public, had they been brought forward in due time.

Amongst these conceptions may be particularised the following :—

1. An improved method of ship-building, both as to ships-of-war and merchantmen, by adding to their strength in framing, and promoting velocity by placing the masts and rigging, and also adding to their durability by preventing in a great measure the attack of dry-rot.

2. Seasoning timber to prevent the dry-rot in ships, churches, and other buildings.

3. To deepen the water on bar-harbours, and in navigable rivers, so as to give easy access to all friends, and to shut out, when necessary, the enemies of our highly favoured land!

4. To build *breakwaters* in any depth, not exceeding twelve or fourteen fathoms water, of materials that will not yield to the surge of the sea, and, when immersed in the briny flood, will become tenacious and durable as *terra-firma*, even as the granite rock.

5. To secure the banks of rivers, [subject to encroachments,] and to support [endangered] buildings of any magnitude.

6. To improve low, wet, barren lands, near tide-flowing rivers, that bear up only mire and dirt, by draining on the ebb and warping on the flood-tide.

7. To draw off the foul and inflammable air from coal-pits and other mines liable to explosion.

8. To lay out new streets, nearly level, over uneven ground, with vaults under them for containing fuel, etc. for the inhabitants, and so arranged as to admit of pipes for gas, water, etc., being laid or altered without molesting the pavements.

9. To improve the hanging of venetian blinds in windows, [and to render them more manageable and useful] for keeping out the sun.

10. To prepare oatmeal for the table by a new method of drying and shelling the corn.

11. "To keep in health" by regimen.

12. To improve the making of *lasts*, so that the boot or shoe may comfortably fit the foot of the wearer.

13. An improved method of pulling down decayed buildings in towns, in order to rebuilding, as also of

making new roads, to the honour of the British nation, the accommodation of trade, commerce, and of the public.

14. Lastly, To beautify the Church and draw man unto it, [not by mere outward architecture and adorning, however admirable,] but by appointing and supporting *faithful pastors* now when the current of prejudice is setting in so strongly against it! "

Some few of my Father's original ideas, on such topics as these, were occasionally elicited in conversation, but, unfortunately, no record was made of them by those immediately in intercourse with him, nor were any papers, generally expository of his views, met with among those amid which this curious and interesting document was found.

SECTION IV.—*Miscellaneous and concluding Notices.*

THE originality of mind, superiority of intelligence and peculiar abilities of the subject of these records, were characteristics yielding much variety of illustration in the foregoing pages.

His peculiar abilities as a whale-fisher, as may have been already inferred, were conspicuous in every department, and in every practical operation connected with the adventurous pursuit. If he could successfully attack, and safely subdue, a vicious and dangerous whale which was working destruction upon others who had assailed it; so he could har-

poon a whale, under circumstances of difficulty or
distance, when no less powerful and expert an arm
could reach it.   In the primary attack, the aim of
the harponeer is to get the boat fairly on the *back* of
the whale, that he may the more effectually bury his
barbed weapon deep in its body; but, as ofttimes
happens, the whale retires from the surface before
the boat can come up to it, and must then be
assailed, if the distance will permit, by the projecting
of the harpoon with an energetic *heave*.   To strike
the retiring or affrighted fish in this manner, with a
weapon, which, with its immediately attached line,
is of the weight of eleven or twelve pounds, is an
operation requiring both strength and skill.   Comparatively few harponeers are able to perform this
important object, effectually, beyond a distance of
twenty to twenty-two feet ; and the distance of four
fathoms, or twenty-four feet, requires superior expert-
ness.   This, however, was an easy range with my
Father ; whilst he has been known to heave his harpoon
with precision and success even as far as twenty-six
or twenty-eight feet.

His management in the urging and furthering of
the general operations of the fishery was sometimes
attended with extraordinary results.   Thus, on one
occasion, during his command of the John of Greenock, he captured thirteen whales in thirty hours,
and flensed five of them, comprising a produce of
about eighty tuns of oil, of the commercial value
(inclusive of the whalebone) of about 3500*l*.!   The ice,

in this case, closing and threatening besetment,
other ships in company urgently made their escape;
my Father, judiciously weighing the risks and probable advantages, determined to abide the issue. He
did so, his ship got beset, but, as he had anticipated,
was soon released, and on the relaxation of the
pressure, just as the ice was opening, whales again
appeared, and he made further important progress
in the fishery!

The originality of talent and tact so observable in
the various records heretofore given, became equally
conspicuous, as occasions offered, in an enlarged and
general scope of application. The following case,
though I do not remember how I learnt it, is so
characteristic of my Father, that I cannot hesitate in
offering it for illustration.

He had a remarkable keenness and power in the
eye, which, in the case referred to, he turned to account with a curious and surprising result. Having
occasion to visit a ship lying in a *tier* in a dock,
he encountered, in his transit across from vessel to
vessel, a fierce and dangerous dog. Though warned
against venturing to cross the deck on which this
formidable looking animal was placed as guardian,
he, relying on the power of the human eye, which
he believed no animal, if its gaze were once fixed,
could bear, determined to venture on the experiment.
Immediately on the dog observing the approach of
an intruder on its domain, it exhibited the most ex-

pressive tokens of the intention to resist; and when my Father put his leg over the bulwark of the contiguous vessel it flew fiercely towards him. Pausing in this position, he strove to catch the eye of the dog, an attempt which for some time it contrived to evade. But at length succeeding so that whenever it glanced towards his face it met his steady, stern, and penetrative gaze, an effect, in the discomposed expression of the creature, became soon observable. Whilst thus obtaining and holding its unwilling look, my Father moved his other leg over and slowly advanced with one foot upon the rail of the guarded vessel,—a movement which was resisted by fierce barking and sundry traverse-like springs, but, withal, an obvious indisposition to attack the being whose eye was so over-awing. Another step forward renewed the display of noise and action, but the stern, fixed look, now perpetually watched, repelled the assailant. He next stood firm on the forbidden deck, and yet was free from attack; he advanced a step, and the dog still bounding from side to side, or forward and backward in front, came no nearer. Another and another step was deliberately, but determinately pushed forward, whilst the dog, repelled by the immovable gaze, yielded the ground. The result, as I have understood, was, that when the dog had been driven entirely across the deck where there happened to be no defence as bulwark, betwixt the rail and the ship's side, my Father sprung a step or two suddenly forward, as if designing, in turn, to become the assailant, when the panic-stricken brute, as suddenly backing, unconsciously passed beneath the railing and fell overboard !

As it has not been our plan in these memorial records to give a regular and general biography, few circumstances in respect to habits on shore, domestic relations, and private life, have been introduced. We may here, however, supply some incidental matters in brief notices.

His habits of life were, in respect to matters of self-indulgence, generally moderate and temperate. At sea, his favourite beverage was tea; and though not connected with any Temperance Society, nor practising total abstinence from stimulating drinks, he was a great tea-drinker. On occasions of long exposure at the mast-head, or after irritation of the throat by much exertion with the speaking-trumpet in giving directions to the men at a distance, when on ice or in boats, he was wont to take what was called an " egg-dram," consisting of a raw egg beat up with a spoonful or two of ardent spirits. This was not unfrequently carried up to him by the steward, and taken in the crow's-nest; but he almost regularly, except at the dinner hour, resorted to tea on each succeeding occasion when refreshment was needed. Under hard and prolonged engagements in fishing, or penetrating the ice, when from twelve to eighteen hours (with but very brief intervals below) might be spent aloft, his call to the steward, as he anticipated a few minutes of respite, was often heard to prepare tea.   And "tea," "tea," some four or five or even six times, betwixt rising from and retiring to his bed, has been the chief orders for refreshment in his hard and protracted exertions.

In character, my Father was patriotic, benevolent, and philanthropic; in temper, quick and passionate, but soon composed, and singularly free from animosity against those with whom he had been at variance, and *most forgiving* to those who had injured him.

He was an enthusiastic admirer of the British Constitution, in Church and State; an ardent loyalist, and a sincere respecter of magisterial authority.   He loved his country, and made neither few nor unexpensive efforts for the public benefit.   On the last renewal of the Whitby Pier Act, when difficulty and opposition were expected, he spent a considerable sum in the engaging of professional assistance with the view to the renewal and improvement of an Act so important to Whitby and the coasting navigation.

His course through life, though of almost uninterrupted prosperity, was not of unmixed quietude. Jealousies and envyings on the part of some; opposition, arising from misconceptions as to what they could not understand, prevailed with others.   But with those amongst whom he was cast, of superior intelligence, he not unfrequently made his way satisfactorily and agreeably.   His personal superior intelligence and originality of conception commended him to the

favourable consideration of many of our most eminent engineers and naval architects, and others professionally engaged in public works. He was well
known to the late Sir John Barrow, and was a rather
frequent visitor at the scientific assemblages at the
house of Sir Joseph Banks, as also many times a
guest at the hospitable table of that distinguished
patron of science.

At all periods of his life, he was well estimated by
many of those whose judgment and superiority were
publicly recognised; and, after his decease, most of
those who had not understood him, received new and
favourable impressions concerning him.

In his regard to religion, there was no special
profession. There was as much freedom from osten-
tation as there was from hypocrisy, which he despised.
As to those things which mankind are prone to fail
in, and as to results in life in which it is found "that
by reason of the frailty of our nature we cannot
always stand upright,"—I never recollect, in his own
case, his excusing them, or expressing views deroga-
tory to Divine Grace, or tending to the *abuse* of its
consoling doctrines. It was most manifest, that his
simple and entire reliance for justification before
God, was in Christ, and Christ alone; and it was
equally manifest that he recognised and held the
duties of Christianity in their broad and practical
bearing, as of grand and indispensable importance
for life and godliness.

But not to anticipate further another opinion, which may serve for a conclusion of these records, I proceed again to quote from Mr. Drew, who, after speaking, in summary, of his life as a seaman and a whale-fisher, noticing very approvingly his improvements in the whale-fishery, and the benefits conferred by his experience and observations on navigation and commerce, proceeds (writing, it will be observed, whilst the subject of his memoir was yet living,) in these commendatory terms:—

"In the career of this man we behold the progress of natural genius and superior talents, surmounting every impediment, and conducting him from a team of oxen and the plough to wealth and reputation, and to the highest honours that the whale-fishery can bestow.

"To this it is pleasing to add, that, instead of imitating the conduct of too many engaged in his profession, ascribing success to *luck* or *fortune*,— Mr. Scoresby, throughout the whole of his dangerous course, acknowledges the overruling Providence of God, and does not forget, though an inhabitant of time, that he has an interest in eternity.

"Of benevolent institutions he is the patron and friend, and the poor of Whitby have experienced his bounty. The diffusion of the truths of Revelation throughout the world has his best wishes and his [most liberal] support. He views Christianity, not merely as a system of ethics, but as possessing a soul-transforming power, which renovates the heart and regulates the life, and as that alone which can make men wise unto salvation."

Reader! If *very* much has been said, in the foregoing pages, in respect of superiority of talent, and energy and originality of mind in the individual whose acts and adventures it has been my object to describe, the statements and facts adduced will, I trust, be found to justify the terms made use of; but if commendations beyond what some might be disposed to yield, have, in any case, been bestowed, or if admiration extending to partiality may have appeared to characterise any of my comments, I would confidently ground my claim on your indulgence in consideration of the circumstance, that the revered subject of these records was

MY FATHER!

Printed by M. MASON, Ivy Lane, Paternoster Row.